INNS & COLONIAL HOMES

OF MARYLAND

Spirits of Romance & Revolution

by
Donna Goldsmith-Day

*"All that mankind has done, thought,
gained or been is lying in magic preservation
in the pages of books."*
Thomas Carlyle

EASTWIND PUBLISHING
Annapolis, Maryland

Preface

For several years I have been researching and considering the writing of this book. Since I was editor of *Dining & Diversions Magazine* for 14 years and associate editor of the Historical and Cultural Journal, *Broad Neck Hundred* four years before that, it seemed that I should compile my experience by writing about historic homes and inns.

The purpose of the book is to inspire people, especially youth, to be more aware of Maryland's heritage, as it was instrumental in the birth of our nation. Youth has several problems in these times, which our generation did not experience. They need heroes other than celebrities and royalty, to base their hopes objectively.

Some of our forefathers were common people who persevered despite tremendous obstacles and at great sacrifice for our freedom. For years after the Revolution, they suffered economically without the trade with the "mother country". They truly did place a great value on independence, not only for themselves, but for future generations.

When young people feel the odds are against them, they can look to these heroes who had faults also as human beings. They can say that they had hard times and terrible opposition, but they, not only got through it, they built magnificent homes which have become national landmarks as testimony to their confidence in this country's ideals for posterity.

Acknowledgements

I appreciate the support of the inn and home owners, who have aided this endeavor by making their financial contributions to which each of their displays are proportionate. They recounted histories in showing their houses and inns to me.

I am thankful to historical societies and architects who have approved the text.

I am grateful to my husband and children for supporting my efforts to complete this book.

I thank my friend, Bob Ackerman, who helped me with computer problems.

I am grateful to Marion E. Warren, of Annapolis, the famous photo-historian, who agreed to do most of the photography and submit his material from the State Archives, a large part of which is his work. He has also traveled the state, photographing the various inns that have requested his services. Other photographs and renderings were submitted by the inns or approved by the colonial home owners.

"History, with its flickering lamp, stumbles along the trail of the past, trying to reconstruct its scenes, to review its echoes and kindle with pale gleams, the passions of former days."
Sir Winston Churchill

Introduction

Maryland is extraordinary for the many homes that are preserved as they were in colonial times. Unlike houses in Williamsburg which have been reproduced, the houses described here are originals. House and Garden tours in this state are fascinating for that reason. Some of these homes have been on tours, but many owners are now reluctant to place their homes on tours for insurance and other reasons. Some of the private owners of these homes as well as inn owners do not have the funds to maintain the houses and are afraid that they may have to sell out to developers. Thus this book may serve in the future as a tour in the reader's imagination.

Old houses are mysterious entities. They give up their family secrets only to the very attentive, who are willing to restore and preserve them. In this book, you will find descriptions of some of the treasures they have discovered and legends of the spirits who inhabit these precious old homes.

Distribution by Eastwind Publishing, Box 1773, Annapolis, Maryland 21404. Telephone 410-721-7987.

ISBN 1-885457-08-1

Contents

A listing of other inns in each county are highlighted with lines above and below their name:

Chef 's recipes from selected inns

Dedication

This book is dedicated to Audrey Davenport who owned the Penwick House Restaurant in Dunkirk for over eighteen years with her husband, Jim.

Mrs. Davenport was definitely a spirit of revolution in Calvert County tourism and a spirit of romance in the beautiful weddings and candlelight dining that she inspired. She also inspired this book, in that she really cared about the historic homes in Calvert and encouraged me to travel the back roads with her map and find them. As her daughter, Penny, so touchingly eulogized her in song at her memorial service, "Calvert was the wind beneath her wings." In all her modesty, she would have told you that her love for the county and its people was a driving force in her every endeavor for the restaurant and for the tourism council on which she served.

"Champ" McCulloch, director of the Council for the State, was the master of ceremonies for her memorial and introduced

Louis Goldstein, Comptroller for the State. His eulogy to her enterprising spirit was followed by that of Mike Miller, President of the State Senate, who said that she believed, "What we are is God's gift to us." He stated that she had been a great wife, mother and entrepreneur. Governor Glendennning's representative, George Williams, said there was no one so stalwart in effort and so hospitable. He said she had a spirit of compassion for everyone.

The Governor's letter stated that she had been a model citizen and had made a selfless donation of time and energy to the State. She was named "Best Travel Person of the Year" for these reasons.

Audrey Davenport also had a lovely, low voice. She was remembered for her fine acting in the Summer Garden Theater. George Williams said that no one had been so consistent and dedicated or had been loved by so many people for her spirit of hospitality.

Champ's wife, Mary Jo McCullock, said

that God give us a bouquet of flowers for friends, and used the analogy of a rose for her good friend, Audrey. She said the rose has utilitarian value for Rosehip jelly and other uses. Audrey was useful as founder of the Southern Maryland Tourism Council, and her stamina and tenacity were vital for the restaurant. She said that she had thorns to protect herself and to exert pressure in her efforts. Her bloom was being a model of hospitality, independence and strength.

She mentioned how much grace she had shown when the barn burned behind the restaurant, when she had been locked in the freezer and when the restaurant, itself, had burned or when her right hand daughter /manager, Vikki had left to marry.

The pastor of All Saints Church said that Audrey would be grateful for the memorial service, as she had been for that of her husband under the Magnolia tree.

St. Mary's County

"Character wants room; it needs perspective, as a great building. We should not require rash explanation... of its action." Ralph Waldo Emerson

St. Mary's County, Maryland's oldest, is one of the few in the state wherein it is still possible to drive for miles without commercial interruption. Civilization's outlet centers and billboards don't yet crowd the highways in many areas. One can still recognize the countryside as it must have been 150 to 200 years ago.

St. Mary's City is much the same as when the brave Calverts and others arrived on The Ark and The Dove.

To get an idea of how ancient, in American terms, the area is, you must depart from the highway, and explore some of the byways and old homes of days of yore.

Old house are enigmatic, keeping their secrets in silence, except for the creaks and thumps in the night that, to the credulous, might indicate ghosts.

Personal and family secrets must be gathered from minute details: scrapings of paint, a talisman walled up fireplaces and secret passages or tunnels. The messages from ancient houses speak of a time when conventions, morals and philosophies were not as they are now.

*"What makes the majesty of the heroes of senate and field?
The consciousness of a train of great victories behind.
There they all stand and shed a united light on the
advancing actor, attended as by an escort of angels.
That is it which throws dignity into Washington's port
and America into Adams' eye. Honor is venerable to
us ...because it is not of today,... it is self-derived and
of an old immaculate pedigree, even if shown in a
young person."* Ralph Waldo Emerson

Governor Leonard Calvert imported ten able men to St. Mary's County, Maryland. Lord Baltimore granted land to Governor Leonard Calvert by single patent on August 30, 1634, according to the "Conditions of the Plantation", published in that year.

The land was then divided into three manors: Trinity Manor 600 acres; Saint Gabrielle's Manor - 900 acres and Saint Michael's Manor - 1500 acres' all contiguous tracts in Saint Michael's Hundred.

The modest 18th century manor house, Bard's Field, is located on Trinity Manor, Ridge Maryland. Bard's Field, 73 A Pratt Rd., Ridge, Maryland 20680. 301-872-5989

Myrtle Point

Myrtle Point Bed and Breakfast, circa 1860, is just over the Thomas Johnson Bridge from Solomons Island in St. Mary's County on the east side of Patuxent Boulevard.

In 1790, it was part of a grant called Piercie's Cost from Charles King to William Carpenter. In 1831, Joseph Cator purchased the land which later belonged to Frances Abell in 1837 as a part of St. Joseph's Manor. When he died, it was turned over to Mary Elizabeth Thompson and in the 1870 census, it was known as Perry's Lot. In 1898 Griffin Hebb sold it to James Fenner Lee, a descendant of Robert E. Lee, who completely remodeled it.

The white frame house is a fine example of a mid-nineteenth century farmhouse looking out on a prime waterway. You can stroll over 20 acres of lovely land and the surrounding gardens.

The house is filled with lovely antiques of the owner's mothers and from abroad. In the dining room is a long pine table, and a china cupboard from Ireland over 200 years old from her great grandmother. In the large living room in a white on white motif, is an armoire with marquetry from Norway. A beautiful foyer greets guest with a cheerful Amish motif, and upstairs are five bedrooms with pristine white carpet.

One room has brass and white beds from Civil War times. Another in blue and white stripes, contains an armoire from Scotland, handsomely carved with a bevelled mirror. Most rooms have a magnificent waterview. The master bedroom is spacious with a welcoming fireplace.

This is an immaculate bed and breakfast with gracious owners, offering a full gourmet country breakfast in the dining room or on the sunny spacious porch. You can enjoy perfect peace and quiet in these congenial surroundings. Just call 301-862-3090 or 800-249-3090 for reservations.

Sketch by Don Swann

Photograph by Marion E. Warren

Cross Manor

Possibly the oldest brick house in the State, Cross Manor stands a few miles from St. Mary s City. The Manor of Cornwaleys Cross was patented to Thomas Cornwaleys, one of the commissioners of Leonard Calvert, on September 8, 1638. He had captured the boat of William Claiborne who had allegedly been privateering. Leonard Calvert, the first Governor of the Colony, had been at odds with Claiborn, since he had been given trading rights to Kent Island. After the victory, he appointed Cornwaleys Deputy Governor.(1)

Corwaleys built the first frame house in the colony, circa 1638 and also a house at Cross Manor.(2)

Resurrection Manor was also deeded to Cornwalleys, circa 1650, and the house was built in 1652. Cornwaleys sold it to Thomas Plowden, a descendant of the Earl of Albion. Sotterley Mansion was built on the northern part of this old foundation.

Regarding Cross Manor, there were three manors, Cornwaley's Cross, St. Elizabeth, each 2,000 acres granted to Thomas Cornwaleys, and Jesuit property on Priest's Point. Cornwaleys built a house at Cross Manor in the mid 17th century.(3)

During the "plundering Time" of Capt. Richard Ingle, the house was cared for by Cuthbert Fenwick, who had accompanied Cornwaleys on the Ark. Richard Ingle held Fenwick prisoner and plundered the entire house, even taking the locks from doors and glass from windows.

In the mid 19th century, it was the home of Captain Randolph Jones, and its wharf was called Grason's Wharf, used as a fueling station during the Civil War. Captain Jones' wife was drowned on the "Steamboat Express," as it was coming from Baltimore to the landing and legend has it that Capt. Jones saw her at the window of the house at the time of her death.

Jones was an active supporter of the Union and on Nov. 11, 1864 The U.S. Tulip blew up because of engine trouble and many of the crew were buried in a locust grove near Cross Manor.(4)

Sotterley Plantation

"Victory, float not forever on the far horizon... Coming from the infinite sea of the future, there will never touch this 'bank and shoal of time' a richer gift... than liberty for man, for woman and for child."   Robert Ingersoll

Sotterley Plantation was named for Sotterley Hall, the family seat of the Satterlees, circa 1066 in Suffolk, England. They were expelled in 1471 from Sotterley Hall for supporting the House of Lancaster in the Wars of the Roses. A family with the name of Playter took the house. In a true example of cause and effect, Satterlee descendants bought Maryland's Sotterley years later after it had been owned and subsequently lost by descendants of the same Playters who had deprived the Satterlees of the English home.(1)

Four huge chimneys divide the house into cottage like portions. In the colonial style, dormer windows accent the long expanse of pitched roof. The building has an ancient fairy tale look. The architecture is unique.

James Bowles, the son of a London merchant, purchased a portion of Resurrection Manor in 1710 and built the center portion where the present sitting room and stair-way hall now exist. The framing he used was crude and could not have survived 200 years. It was fortunate for posterity that when he remodeled he reinforced the original construction. Yet, a portion of the sturdy cedar post construction is visible today inside the west wall sitting room.(2)

Building materials listed in Bowles inventory became incorporated into the plantation house after his death, probably because Bowles had plans for further remodeling. They were carried out when his widow married George Plater in 1729. Here, enters the "Playter" connection.

Her husband served Maryland as collector of customs, member of governor's council and Provincial Secretary. He continued enlarging of the simple three-room plantation house, and brought the estate into the Plater family where it remained for nearly 100 years and four generations of George Platers.

George Plater III expanded it to the size it is today. As naval officer of the Patuxent, member of the Maryland House of Delegates, member of the Continental Congress, President of the Maryland Senate and sixth Governor of Maryland, he was Sotterley's most distinguished resident. He was possibly buried on Sotterley's grounds.

One daughter married Francis Scott Key's uncle in the garden on the Fourth of July. Her scrawled signature "Eliz Key" is on a pane of glass in the drawing room window.(3)

A story told by a slave named Harriet Brown concerns a woodcarver named Richard Boulton. Boulton was an indentured servant. The master workman had difficulty drafting a model of the stairway in the house. When dinner was announced all went in but Boulton, who, as an indentured servant should not have sat at table with his master. He employed himself by drawing a model of the proposed staircase. When his master saw the fine ingenuity of the drawing of the Chinese Chippendale staircase, he said that anyone who could do such work should be a free man, the story is told.(4)

George Plater, the builder's grandson lost Sotterley in a game of chance. The story is told that after a series of mortgages failed to alleviate his financial straits, young Plater in 1822, staked his title to Sotterley on a game of dice.

Colonel Somerville's sale in 1822 of most of the plantation brought the mansion into the hands of Thomas Barber and his stepdaughter, Emeline Dallam, who married Dr. Walter Briscoe in 1826, beginning another century of occupation by a single family.(5)

A secret passage between the sitting room and bedroom above was apparently of good use to hide Dr. Briscoe, a confederate sympathizer, when the Army of the Potomac encamped on the plantation grounds.

In 1910, Herbert Satterlee, a New York lawyer bought Sotterley as a retreat from Washington where he was serving as Under Secretary of the Navy. He studied its history, restored it to its 18th century appearance and underpinned the structure with concrete footing. Between 1910 and 1940, he, his wife and two daughters lived without central heat and electricity, used the 18th century garden privy and carried candles in order to preserve its authenticity.(6)

The house is open to the public June 1 to Sept. 30. Phone 301-373-2280.

St. Michael's Manor

In St. Mary's County, just a mile from Scotland near Point Lookout is St. Michael's Manor near an inlet of the Chesapeake Bay. The original estate was one of three manors south of Smith Creek granted to Governor Leonard Calvert in 1639, covering 1,000 acres. It included all of Scotland and Point Lookout and Scotland Beach. St. Michaels was the first manor.

St. Michaels Manor was built by James I. Richardson about 1805. There is a brick in the house, formerly in a cornerstone, now in Capt. and Mrs. Dick's private portion, that reads:" J.I.R. 1805". Other families who have owned the house are the Langleys, Milburns, Williamson Smiths and the Viseks.

It was purchased in 1982 by Captain and Mrs. Joseph I. Dick and made into a bed & breakfast through renovations every year. The Dicks also have a winery on the property and regale their guests with excellent vintages.

At one time the house laid vacant for 17 years, and some psychics and other intuitive family members sense the presence of spirits, having tea parties or ghosts of civil War Soldiers who died at the Union Camp at Point Lookout, nearby.

People who lived there in 1941 say that cannon balls were near the fireplace which had been in the living room before the open central hall was removed and the living room was enlarged. This room is charming with an antique organ from 1880, original blue and white fireplaces, needlepoint seats and a lovely throw from Scotland. A built in cupboard has the original bubble glass.

Mrs. Dicks plays a pump organ on weekends at St. Mary's Chapel of Ease, and has an organ and a piano from years gone by in this room.

A galley kitchen is down the hall near a gracious dining room and upstairs are several beautifully appointed guest rooms replete with Mrs. Dick's mother's antiques. An Amish Room looks out on the water.

In another room, a bed from Point Lookout and antique quilts lend more authenticity, while spacious baths remind one that this is a true country inn. Detailed panelling on the top floors may indicate that these were the Richardson's living quarters. Call 301-872-4025 for reservations, wine tastings or to enjoy the September festival.

Charles County

"Could the mist of antiquity be cleared away, it is probable that the [Greeks and Romans] would admire us, rather than we them. America has surmounted a greater variety of difficulties than... any other people, in the same space of time, and has replenished the world with more useful knowledge and sounder maxims of civil government than were ever produced in any age before." *Thomas Paine*

Stone Mansion

Charles County is even more replete with natural stretches of landscape than parts of St. Mary's. It is also easily accessible from Annapolis by taking 97 to 301 to 205, eliminating the commercial area of Waldorf. You will find the Mansion of Governor Thomas Stone three miles from La Plata on the west side of Rose Hill Road. Stone was a signer of the Declaration of Independence, who had his city home in the Peggy Stewart House in Annapolis but was born in Charles County. His younger brother, John Hoskins Stone, also became Governor of Maryland and returned to his native county.(1)

Thomas Stone served as State Senator and as a delegate to Congress under the Articles of Confederation. He declined to be a delegate to the Continental Congress because of failing health and died in 1787.(2)

The National Park Service operates it as The Thomas Stone Historic Site. Its five parts are arranged in an arch. The central section is brick with a gambrel roof and to the east is a small frame and one-half storey gambrel roof structure.(3) The site is open to the public. Call 301-934-0961.

Dr. Samuel Mudd House

"The way for a young man to rise is to improve himself, never suspecting that anybody wishes to hinder him. Allow me to assure you that suspicion and jealousy never did help any man... Thus let bygones be bygones: let past differences as nothing be; and with steady eye on the real issue let us reinaugurate the good old 'central ideas' of the Republic... that 'all men are created equal'." *Abraham Lincoln*

The Dr. Samuel Mudd House, circa 1830, now on the National Register, was restored because Dr. Mudd's granddaughter believed that the spirit of her grandfather wanted to be vindicated.

Dr. Mudd was implicated in the assassination of President Lincoln, since he had treated the injured leg of John Wilkes Booth, which his Hippocratic Oath obligated him to do.

On April 15, 1865 at 4 a.m. he rose from sleeping at the Mudd farmhouse and went to answer a knock on his door. Dr. Mudd did not recognize John Wilkes Booth, because Booth was in disguise.

Dr. Mudd was tried and convicted by a military court then, sentenced to life imprisonment at Fort Jefferson on Dry Tortugas Island, Florida.

He was pardoned by President Andrew Johnson four years later, following a request for the doctor's release, signed by all prisoners and wardens in appreciation for Mudd's aid in a yellow fever epidemic.

He died in 1883, his reputation damaged.

For the next century his family members tried to clear his name and President Carter also publicly proclaimed his belief in Dr. Mudd's innocence.

Louise Mudd Arehart has always been interested in clearing her grandfather's name. She was given a push in that direction by his spirit, which she met in the hallway of her own house about thirty years ago. Then, she began to see him from afar in a white shirt with rolled up sleeves. Finally, she recognized the man as her grandfather. She organized the Committee for the Restoration of the Samuel A. Mudd House. Call 301-934-8464 for tours.

Shady Oaks of Serenity

Shady Oaks of Serenity is a beautiful bed and breakfast inn of Charles County. From Baltimore or Annapolis, it is just a short drive up 97 to 301 to 205. Located off Rt. 5, it is accessible by turning right on Oliver Shop Road and left on Oaks Road. Turn right at the Serenity Woods sign and you will find it on your left at 7490 Serenity Drive. The area is definitely serene with rolling front lawns amidst tall old trees. It is not far from the Amish country of St. Mary's County, and the house is decorated with pictures of the Amish and even an Amish hat in the guest room on the main floor, which has a private bath, king size bed and self service bar. A room with a double bed and one with twin beds are upstairs with a shared bath.

The house is a Georgian Victorian with a wide columned portico and is the first B & B in Charles County. Surrounded by historic homes, it is near the famous home off Rt. 205 of Dr. Samuel Mudd, who treated John Wilkes Booth during his escape after the assassination of President Lincoln. Not far away is the Thomas stone National Historic site in Port Tobacco. Thomas Stone was a signer of the Declaration of Independence.

Kathy Kazimer and retired husband, Gene, used their building talents to change the home from a simple wooden frame to a large, stately house with two family rooms, fireplace, patio, four upstairs bedrooms, and a 3 car garage.

Visitors are welcome to gather in the sitting room or large deck. This is a sunny cheerful spot for breakfast or high tea, which are included in the reasonable overnight rate. Please call 301-923-8864 or 800-597-0924 for reservations.

Baltimore City

The renaissance of Baltimore City is remarkable, but not all for the best from an architectural perspective. During the turn-of-the-century some noteworthy old homes were destroyed. Still, many of its stately old mansions have been preserved.

The new Harbor Place offers the National Aquarium, Science Center and historic districts boast world class art galleries. One of a kind museums include the Museum of Industry, the Flag House, where our national flag was sewn, and living history museums such as the 1840 House.

The ethnic diversity of Baltimore makes the city a wonderful maze of exciting restaurants. Cultural attractions include the Meyerhof Symphony Hall and Lyric Opera, and the Camden Yards Stadium.

The light rail takes you from the city to Baltimore's beautiful mansions with ease and comfort, as the metro subway system takes you around town.

Distinguished Accommodations

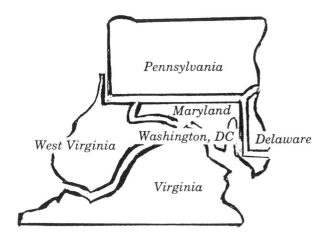

Distinguished Accommodations in the Potomac Region offers accommodations of the highest quality. Each listed accommodation has been subjected to the most discerning inquiry to assure your complete satisfaction.

The service will locate luxury facilities that fulfill your most specific needs. Amenities may include fireplace, jacuzzi, special interests, business needs, or quiet relaxation.

DAPR is an affiliate of Amanda's Bed & Breakfast Reservation Service, satisfying a discriminating clientele for over a decade Call 410-225-000 /.

Sketch by Don Swann

Mount Clare Mansion

Mount Clare Mansion was named after Dr. Charles Carroll's sister, Mary Clare, and his grandmother, Clare Dunn.

A renowned Irishman, Dr. Charles Carroll, called "the Immigrant", a distant cousin of "the settler" arrived in the colonies in 1715 and died in 1755. During his life he gained one of the six greatest fortunes in the colonies.(1)

His son, Charles Carroll the Barrister, inherited most of his wealth. In 1756, he began to build a manor house on one of his father's lands, the "Georgian Plantation", near Baltimore along the Patapsco River.

Today, it is situated in what is now Carroll Park in southwest Baltimore amidst a grove of English elms, planted by Generals Washington and Lafayette and Charles Carroll over 200 years ago.(2)

The house has a stable in which weddings are held.

The Barrister, educated in law at Middle Temple in London, was responsible in part for writing the Maryland Declaration of Rights and the State Constitution. Later he was asked to be Chief Judge of Maryland but declined because of chronic malaria.

Because it was near a prominent supply route during the Revolution, Mount Clare hosted important generals. Washington corresponded with Mrs. Carroll about her orangery and the one he hoped to build at Mount Vernon. (3)

Mount Clare is the oldest pre-Revolutionary house in Baltimore and is open to the public. Call 410-837-3262.

Bauernschmidt Manor

Bauernschmidt Manor Bed and Breakfast at 2316 Baurernschmidt Dr. in Baltimore is a home of historic significance as the famous summer residence of Frederick and Agnes (nee Wehr) Bauernschmidt. The Bauernschmidt name is a prominent family name in Baltimore brewing history. George Bauernschmidt, Frederick's father, began brewing beer in Baltimore in 1873, building an empire that he sold to a trust in 1898 for a million dollars. Frederick objected to this sale and started a competing brewery, eventually destroying the trust financially.

George and Margaret Bauernschmidt had four sons. They were John (1863-1926), Frederick(1864-1933), George, Jr. (1868-1892) and William (1874-1934). It was William who married Marie O. Von Hattersheim (1875-1962), the famous "Mrs. B.", who was instrumental in city public school reform during the 1920's and 30's. She once said, "You have to handle politicians with kid gloves, and you have to have a rock in your mitt." She retired from political life, although she never held public office, around 1948 at age 73. She is the Bauernschmidt most people remember.

George and Margaret also had three daughters: Sarah (1865-1941), Elizabeth (1871-1924) and Emily (1873-1911).

Bauernschmidt Manor, designed by Robert C. Ullrich, was built in 1910. The site was originally called "Planters paradise", a name continued by Frederick and Agnes. They lived at "Planters Paradise" estate the months of June, July and August. The site was also used to rest the Belgian horses that pulled the brewery's beer wagons. Agnes sold the estate with its house, 44 acres and "out buildings" at auction ten years after the 1933 death of her husband.

Frederick had made his fortune in the brewing

business, purportedly building the American Brewery on Gay St. into one of the largest in the world. His unique logo was imbedded on Bauernschmidt beer bottles (used only during Prohibition) and is also over the second floor porch door of the Manor.

Childless, Frederick and Agnes gave generously during their lifetime and in their bequests. They were humble about their many philanthropies, preferring not to speak of them. Their philosophy is perhaps summed up best on the stained glass window in their mausoleum that reads:" Faith, Hope and Charity, of these the greatest is Charity".(The Bible)

The large, spacious B & B has three suites: The Bauernschmidt Suite with a king-size, four-poster bed, fireplace and jacuzzi. The Baltimore suite with king-size brass bed and a 5 foot claw foot tub. The Suite Agnes with a queen size bed, fireplace and steam shower.

A full gourmet or Continental breakfast is included. All suites have private baths, central air, remote color T.V. and C.D. player. Other amenities include an in-ground swimming pool, pool table and cozy sitting areas throughout the house. Weddings and receptions are held at this lovely setting. Your Hosts: Will and Sue Gerard

Reservations required 410-687-ABED (2233) or 1-800-735-6360.

Ballestone Manor

Jefferson's Character of Washington: "His mind was powerful, his penetration strong though not as acute as that of a Newton, Bacon or Locke. His integrity was most pure, his justice of the most inflexible... no motives of interest, friendship or hatred, being able to bias his decision. He was in every sense a wise a good and great man. He often declared to me that he considered our new constitution as an experiment on the practicability of republican government, and with what dose of liberty man could be trusted for his own good; that he was determined the experiment should have a fair trial, and would lose the l ast drop of his blood in support of it." Thomas Jefferson

---

Ballestone Manor, next to the Rocky Point Golf Course in Essex, was originally a grant in 1659 to William Ball, the maternal great grandfather of George Washington from Cecil Calvert. A Virginian, Ball viewed the site as an investment and sold it in 1678. Although he never lived in Maryland, he gave his name to the parcel of land, and it became known as "Baliston".

Prior to the Revolution, the Thomas Stansbury family acquired a majority of the 1659 land grant. Their son, Dixon, is believed to have built the nucleus of the present house in the 1780's.

The Leakin family purchased the property in 1819 and in 1855, Edward Miller became the next owner.

His family owned it until 1969, when Baltimore County purchased the property to develop as a park.

The deserted Ballestone house had fallen victim to vandals and was severely damaged. The Heritage Society of Essex and Middle river petitioned Baltimore County to preserve the structure. In 1977, Ballestone was opened for visitors.

Today the site is administered by the Ballestone Preservation Society. The house offers period rooms, depicting each phase of its development.

A Federal period dining room, circa 1780-1820, begins the tour which leads the visitor through the next 100 years of American decorative arts. A print of George Washington is in the room and a family scene of the Washingtons hangs in the hall.

A Victorian parlor circa 1840-1875 is set for tea with groups of furniture, made of genuine horse hair. There is a copy of an ingrain carpet as well as a draped portrait of Abraham Lincoln. Upstairs is an Empire bedroom, circa 1820-1840. A museum exhibit room displays varied changing exhibits.

Seasonal special events are planned. In the fall, a living history weekend is held. In winter, period decorations fill the house for a delightful annual Holly Tour. In spring, an opening ceremony features a tea plate luncheon. In summer, the house is open for Regular Summer Hours: Sundays 2 - 5 p.m. Visitors are welcome at other times by special appointment. Call 410-887-0218.

Gramercy Mansion

---

*"Those who govern, [being busy], do not usually like to
take the trouble of considering and carrying into
execution new projects. The best public measures are
therefore seldom adopted from previous wisdom, but
forced by the occasion." "Wealth and content are not
always bedfellows. Wise men learn by others' harms;
Fools by their own."*   Benjamin Franklin

Gramercy is a majestic English Tudor mansion on
45 acres in Green Spring Valley near Baltimore, providing elegant living in turn-of-the-century style. The
26 room historic manor, now a bed and breakfast at
1400 Green Spring Valley Rd., offers large fireplaces,
spacious rooms, terraces, porches, a pool and tennis
courts. A large carriage house is available for educa-
tional seminars or overflow from weddings hosted at
the great house. The property is an organic farm,
specializing in culinary herbs and specialty produce.

The historical legacy is through its builder. Alexander J. Cassatt bought the property, a parcel of
General Felix Angus' "Nacirema", patented in 1800.
He built the house to celebrate the marriage of his
daughter, Eliza, to W. Plunkett Stewart in 1902.

For some reason, he then offered his son-in-law a
job in Philadelphia. Stewart was a Baltimore native,
but perhaps Eliza was homesick.

Five years after their move from Gramercy, a
strange tragedy struck. Their nine year old son told
his mother he had seen an angel who said it would
take him away. He did die that night without appar-
ent cause. In his memory, the Stewarts added a Tiffany stained glass window in St. Thomas Church
nearby.

In 1911, Benjamin H. Brewster, Jr. descendant of
Ben Franklin and son of the U.S. Attorney General
under President Arthur moved into the house and
the family lived there for 30 years.

It is said that his wife, who piloted in an open
cockpit, haunts the third floor.

The Hunt Room, recently restored, offers a king
size postered bed, marble tiled bath and jacuzzi. A
forest green motif and hunt trophies, such as a
whimsical stag's head with hat, carry out the sport-
ing theme. Aphrodite's Retreat is the feminine complement with Oriental carpets, French antiques,
mauve tones and lace.

Aunt Mary's Suite, named after Mary Cassatt,
displays her paintings. Designed during the
Decorator's Show House, it offers a Victorian canopy
bed and ornate dressing table, fireplace and claw foot
soaking tub.

The Ambassador's Room is splendidly romantic
with chandelier and king size bed, warmed by a fireplace and complemented by a bath with whirlpool
tub. Fresh flowers in each room, robes, tea service,
sodas and snacks are special amenities.

The Blue Garden Suite features a spacious sun
porch for surveying gardens, and a bedroom with
Louis XIV furnishings and shirred moire ceiling. Another room offers a fireplace, bed and game table.
Three nicely furnished single rooms share hall baths.

The intricately carved grand staircase makes weddings memorable, as the bride walks down to the
grand hall. A library to the right of the foyer offers
comfortable seating and a pump organ with adjacent
bar room. It looks into another spacious room with a
grand piano and tall windows, giving out onto the
gardens.

To the left, is a large parlor. A shirred cloth ceiling
with low beams is spectacular over tables set for a
wedding. A nearby conservatory room for gourmet
breakfasts looks out on a patio.

In this pristine setting, guests stroll through
woodland trails near sparkling streams amid organic
herb and flower gardens. Call 410-486-2405 for reservations.

Sketch by Don Swann

Hampton Mansion

Rebecca Dorsey Ridgely, when she had married Captain Charles Ridgely, arrived at her home and fell immediately to prayer, because it was so beautiful. It is one of the most ornate mansions built during the post Revolutionary War period. On Hampton Lane off Dulaney Valley Road in Towson, it is open to the public.(1)

At one time it was a 24,00 acre estate. The original tract of 1500 aces was purchased in 1745 by the prominent Ridgely family. Iron ore deposits were found nearby and the Ridgelys established the Northampton Ironworks, which supplied military supplies to patriot forces during the Revolution.

With no direct descendants at the time of his death, the Captain willed Hampton to his nephew, Charles Ridgely Carnan, with the proviso that he change his name to Charles Carnan Ridgely.

Charles Carnan Ridgely, who assumed Hampton in 1790, married Rebecca's sister, Priscilla Dorsey. He became a representative in the Maryland General Assembly from 1790-1795, a Senator from 1796-1800 and Governor of Maryland from 1815-1818.(2)

Hampton is a combination of classical design and five-part Georgian plan. It was probably designed by Captain Ridgely and his chief carpenter, Jehu Howell, who suggested the cupola surmounting the roof.(3)

The main house was completed in 1790. The formal gardens contain beautiful trees including exotic specimens, plus many outbuildings.(4)

The house is open to the public with tours by Historic Hampton. Call 410-962-0688.

Bed & Breakfast on the Park

If you desire complete privacy in the city, visit Bed and Breakfast on the Park at 1315 John Street in the historic Bolton Hill section of Baltimore. The brick town house, circa 1880, faces the first street park established in Baltimore and is close to many attractions of interest to the visitor; the Lyric Opera House, the Myerhoff Symphony Hall, the Maryland Historical Society, the Maryland Institute College of Art, the University of Baltimore, and Antique Row.

The spacious bed-setting room with its attached bath and kitchenette provides a sequestered hideaway for your time spent in Baltimore be it for business, a honeymoon, a family vacation, or just to "get away from it all". Furnishings are antiques and other period pieces and include a king-size bed and loveseat sofa-bed. A playpen/crib is available for those traveling with a small child.

The bath has a tub/shower; and the refrigerator is stocked with fresh fruit, milk, juice and other breakfast foods to eat at your leisure at the drop-leaf table or in the bricked garden down a private hallway. Features include a remote-control television, bedside telephone, air conditioning, and a separate thermostat to regulate the heat. Arrangements may be made to use the laundry facilities.

Three blocks away is the light rail stop and its direct line to Orioles Park at Camden Yards and near Harbor Place; five blocks away is the Metro leading to downtown Baltimore and the Johns Hopkins Hospital; the restored Pennsylvania railroad station with its Amtrack services is just five blocks away as well. The Bolton Hill Swim and Tennis Club is available to guests in season and is a short three blocks away from John Street.

Your charming hosts, George and Barbara Elder, in their quarters just above the guest accommodations, will add to the pleasure you are sure to enjoy at Bed and Breakfast on the Park.

Call them at 410-523-0576 for reservations.

Ann Street B & B
124 S. Ann Street
Baltimore, Md.
410 342-5883

Calvert County

Maryland's colonial heritage is evident in unspoiled Calvert County, founded in 1654. In 1632, King Charles I granted a large territory north of the Potomac River to Sir George Calvert, who left its naming to Charles. The king proposed naming it in honor of his Queen, Henrietta Maria, and suggested Maryland.

George's son, Leonard, established the platinate on March 25, 1634 at St. Mary's City. Anne Arundel County was named after his lovely wife, while Calvert County is named for his family.

Explore the majestic Calvert Cliffs with 15 million years of prehistoric fossils at Calvert Cliffs State Park. Flag Ponds Nature Park offers sandy beaches, freshwater ponds and primeval forests. Battle Creek Cyress Swamp Sanctuary off Rt. 506 is one of the northernmost stands of Bald Cypress in North America. Tour the area where Saber-toothed tigers once roamed.

In Solomons Island at the Calvert Marine Museum, explore the lore of the Bay, cruise the harbor in a bugeye and delight as otters play. Licensed captains offer fishing trips. Jefferson Patterson Park and Museum, on the Patuxent River and St. Leonard Creek, is an archeological preserve, which chronicles over 9,000 years of Maryland's history. It overlooks the site of the Battle of St. Leonard's Creek where Cmd. Joshua Barney engaged the British during the War of 1812.

In Chesapeake Beach, enjoy not only sandy beaches but also the Chesapeake Beach Railway Company's collection of photos and artifacts at the Railway Museum, dating from 1898. Call 410-342-5883.

Preston On Patuxent

In the mid 17th century the important men of the Colony gathered at a small house in Lusby called Preston On Patuxent, as it was the capital of Maryland from 1654 to 1659. All the records from St. Mary's City were brought here when the proprietary government was deposed in 1654.(1) Erected in 1650, it is one of the earliest Colonial homes in the State. The land was patented in 1652 to Richard Preston, called "the Great Quaker" by Governor Charles Calvert. His grandson was Mayor of Philadelphia.

In 1676, it was purchased by Captain Richard Ladd who left no descendants and left it to Christ's Church in his will. It was later acquired by a branch of the Johnson family. Louisa Catherine Johnson, niece of three times Governor Thomas Johnson married President John Quincy Adams.(2)

Hulbert Footnare who wrote the novel, *Charles' Gift,* lived in the house and wrote about the interior.

He stated that one room on the top floor had a fireplace and only one original door remained.(3)

Preston-On-Patuxent has a huge room which stretches the entire length of the original building. At either end are brick fireplaces with remarkable round arches. On the right of the north fireplace are winding steps, leading to the second floor.

Bowens Inn

Celebrating a reputation for fine food and hospitality since 1918, Bowen's Inn rises above the Solomons skyline. Bowen's Inn has been a family business since George M. (Mort) Bowen built the original old White Inn, located in front of the present structure. The Inn featured rooms at $1.00 per person and All-You-Can-Eat meals for $1.00. For many years the business also handled fishing accommodations with a fleet of eight Bay-built charter boats. A 4-hour fishing trip cost $5.00.

The bar building was built in 1828 as an annex, with 6 rooms upstairs and 6 rooms downstairs. With the repeal of Prohibition in the 1930's the annex was converted to a bar. During World War II the second floor was the Officer's bar. At that time the Island was located in the center of 3 US Naval operations; Amphibious Training Center, Mine test, and Patuxent River Naval Air Station. The "new" Inn building, completed in 1937, had 40 rooms and a restaurant with a full menu featuring local seafood dishes. The present restoration and renovation venture will provide the Inn with modern accommodations.

All "old" places are supposed to have a ghost, and Bowen's Inn has its stories too. One evening, while attending a party at the Inn, a charter boat Captain's daughter went up stairs to the Ladies'Room. Returning breathlessly, she told of seeing a lady in a white dress rush past her. Another time, a worker hurried down the stairs, two at a time. He had also seen "a woman in white". No one knows who the 'lady' is, but the stories don't frighten the locals. You will find many local residents savoring the Prime Rib, a specialty of Bowen's Inn, while enjoying the activity in Solomons Inner Harbor. 410-326-9814.

Grey Fox Inn

Grey Fox Inn, on the main street of Solomons Island across from Solomon's Pier Restaurant was the home of a physician in the early 1900's. Upstairs are two guest rooms in Victorian motifs, one in tan tones with masculine accents, a sofa and chair, and the other in blue hues with an antique dresser and queen sized brass bed. An efficiency looks out on the water to the back, and the front bedrooms look out upon the beautiful Bay.

Dr. Coster, for whom Coster Road near the town is named, had his office in the room to the left of the front door and lived in the house in the early 1900's. These lower rooms now house a charming shop of collectibles. Tee shirts with waterfowl and bay view panoramas are printed here before your eyes. One room is devoted to a Christmas collectible niche, offering hand crafted items and hand painted decoys. Another room is occupied by a Maryland artist, offering paintings and sketches of Solomons Island.

Don't be surprised if you see an occasional vision of a white dog switching his tail. This mystery of the house was first noticed by the owner, Evelyn, while moving into the shop. She thought she saw something white in the doorway and blamed it on being tired from over work. Several months later, her assistant asked her if she ever saw a white streak in the doorway. Evelyn told her about seeing the swishing white form.

Finally, in preparation for this book, Evelyn asked old time residents of the island whether Dr. and Mrs. Coster had had a dog. She learned that they did, in fact, have a white poodle, named "Pudgeons".

Recently, a customer came into the shop looking somewhat mystified. She asked if a ghost might inhabit the house, since she felt a strange feeling against her legs as she stood by the door. Evelyn just smiled enigmatically, thinking that "pudgeons" had returned once again to his beloved home. Call 410-326-6826.

Guy Hardesty Home

The Guy Hardesty Home at 4480 Hardesty Rd. in Huntingtown, Md. is on the Historic Register. A deed shows the Guy Hardesty acquired this property in November of 1906 (Liber GWD7/110.) He was 21 years of age at the time, and one would not expect that he built the house. The house also probably contains the elements of an earlier structure.

This farmhouse is important for the late Victorian elements it displays, a gingerbread front porch with Eastlake-type front door. The brown shingles cover the original German siding.

The west wing has two dormers that show concern for classicism as do deep cornices on the gables and the pediment moldings on the front door.

The interior features a formal living room, dining room and family room, kitchen, bath and sunporches on the main level, plus three bedrooms and a bath on the upper level. An elegant stairway rises from the foyer and a maids stairway from the kitchen area.

Old Field Inn

Old Field Inn on Rt. 765 in the historic district of Prince Frederick is an elegant two storey house with almost a century of history. Built in the last decade of the 19th century by Judge John Parran Briscoe, Old Field was named after the tract of land on which it was built, Williams Old Field, which was no longer suitable for planting. When Judge Briscoe moved his family to Baltimore in the early 1920's, the house stood vacant for years. In 1927, Old Field became the home of Dr. Everard Briscoe, his wife, Betty Worthington Briscoe, and their children. One of the first physicians in Calvert County to hold regular office hours, Dr. Briscoe practiced medicine from Old field for 21 years, until his death in 1944.

Dr. Briscoe's widow continued to live at Old Field, and established herself as one of Calvert County's leading citizens. A gracious hostess, always welcoming many guests, she was a horticulturist and planted beautiful gardens.

Today, the Old Field Inn is a restaurant. Two lovely dining rooms are at either side of the hallway foyer with a relaxing lounge at the back. Old Field serves luncheon Wednesday through Friday 11:30 a.m. - 2 p.m. and dinner each day from 5 p.m.

Enjoy a Seafood Sampler for two, with Clams Casino, Fire Island Shrimp, Stuffed Mushrooms and Oysters Rockefeller. Other starters include Escargot in Puff Pastry, Fried Calamari, Cheese Beignets with raspberry sauce, and French Onion Gratinee or Cream of Crab soup.

Select from such innovative entrees as Veal Wellington, with hunter sauce, Veal Oscar, Pork Chops with wild mushroom compote, Breast of Chicken en Croute with crabmeat, sour cream and cheddar cheese, or Chicken Dijon, grilled with cheeses.

Seafood Entrees include Honey Nut Shrimp, Stuffed Rainbow Trout, North Atlantic Salmon or Salmon Parmesan and twin Lobster Tails. Surf & Turf combines a lobster tail with hand cut filet, also served solo, bacon wrapped with bearnaise or with bleu cheese crumb crust with beurre rouge sauce. A Rack of Lamb is served with mint sauce and Prime Rib of Beef with horseradish sauce upon request. Blackened N. Y. Strip, Rib Eye and Steak au Poivre Flambeed in brandy top off the beef specialties of the owner/chef.

Save room for delectibles on the tempting dessert tray and plan your next special occasion at this enchanting home, turned restaurant. Call 410-535-1054 or 301-855-1054 for reservations.

Old Field's Layered Blueberry Pie
1 unbaked pie crust	1 cup chopped pecans
4 ounces cream cheese	2 cups powdered sugar
6 ounces Cool Whip	1/2 teaspoon vanilla extract
1 16 oz can blueberry pie filling or	
half of the following recipe:	

1 quart blueberries   1 cup sugar
3 tbs. cornstarch   1/8 tsp. salt
1 tbs. butter

Wash and drain berries. Combine sugar, ornstarch, salt, water and all but 1 cup of berries. Cook and stir over low heat until thick. Add the rest of the blueberries and butter. Cool completely.

Preheat oven to 350 degrees. Place pecans in the bottom of pie crust. Bake until crust is golden brown. Cool completely. Beat cream cheese with sugar until smooth. Fold in Cool Whip and vanilla extract (You may substitute 3/4 cup heavy cream whipped with 1 cup powdered sugar.) Then mix in 6 oz. cream cheese until smooth.) Pour mixture over cooled crust and level. Top cream layer with blueberry pie filling. Chill and serve.

Rousby Hall

One of Calvert's most historic properties, Rousby Hall was built circa 1730 by order of King Charles and was probably Maryland's first customs house. It was in all probability the office of John Rousby II, the builder of Rousby Hall's first house.

Rousby Hall was the estate of John Rousby II, a lawyer and custom's keeper   the nephew of Christopher Rousby, the first person appointed King's Collector of Customs for the Patuxent District. He was appointed to this office and held it until his death in 1744.

The original plantation was patented ln 1652 and subdivided in 1706. John Rousby purchased 2500 acres from the Bourne family in 1706, who had acquired the title to 5,000 acres. At the failure of the original grantee Edward Eltonhead, to bring the required fifty people to America, the property "escheated" to the King and was regranted to Henry Sewall, Esq. on October 20, 1663. The Bourne's sold 2.500 acres of half of the property to John Rousby II.

The first John Rousby had died in February 1686 on the way to or back from England where he was seeking justice from the King for the death of his elder brother, Christopher, at the hands of Colonel George Talbot.

The third Lord Baltimore recommended Christopher to his position as collector of the customs. Christopher Rousby was stabbed to death aboard the ship, "Quaker Ketch" by Col. George Talbot, cousin of Lord Baltimore, who had served as Deputy Governor of Maryland. He was imprisoned aboard ship, then sent to a Virginia jail to await hanging, when he was set free by his wife. He was recaptured, but King Charles, responding to Lord Baltimore's plea, allowed Talbot to return to England(4).

John Rousby inherited his brother's estate which later became the 6800 acre Patuxent Naval Air Station. When John died his son John II held both properties, Christopher Rousby's home, known as Susquehana, now duplicated in Michigan, and Rousby Hall. The graves of Christopher and John were also moved to Michigan. Records indicate that John the II built Rousby Hall in 1730, a five-bedroom brick Georgian Colonial house with a ball room, a barn, meat house and office (custom house), all built in brick, surrounded by a six foot high wall and had gardens and terraces leading to the Patuxent River. Excavations in 1984 revealed a brick underground tunnel leading from the river to the old mansion. In 1995, excavations began at the old barn site and the original foundations were found. This property also included what is now referred to as Solomons Island. It is said by some authorities that the large old house on the Island belonged to the caretaker at Rousby Hall. *(as told to me by Mr. Elliot Kocen, the owner of Rousby Hall)*

At the death of his father, John Rousby III inherited Rousby Hall and lived there until his death on January 28, 1750. He left the widow, Anne Rousby, and daughter Elizabeth. Anne eventually married William Fitzhugh after a long and fabled courtship. He was one of America's wealthiest men and a probable friend of Lawrence Washington, elder brother of our first President. The two served together under Admiral Vernon at Carthegena.

While William Fitzhugh lived at Rousby Hall many parties were held there, some went on for days. In fact, the last royal Governor of Maryland, Governor Robert Eden, enjoyed Christmas 1770 at Rousby Hall. The Maryland Gazette of October 17, 1754 mentions that Colonel Sharp, while on his way to Virginia, enjoyed the "Southern Hospitality" of Rousby Hall.

The British destroyed the original Rousby Hall because William Fitzhugh, then an officer in the Continental Army and owner of Rousby Hall, refused to supply three British "schooners" with food and water. They bombarded the house and sent forty marines ashore to burn down what was not blown up. They presumably left the Custom House because they felt they belonged to the King. (as told to me by Mr. Kocen)

Tax records indicate a white house on the property in 1783, about three years after the destruction of the Rousby Hall mansion on November 7, 1780, noted to the commanding general in Annapolis and in the Annapolis Gazette. The Kocens excavated under the dining room of the white structure and found the burnt brick remnants of the old structure, including its foundations, which lead underground almost to the Customs House.

There is no evidence that William Fitzhugh tried to rebuild the mansion.

In this century Rousby Hall and its cottage were beautifully restored by several individuals. In 1940, Mrs. Eble, from Baltimore, shored up, plumbed and wired the old house. She eventually sold it to a retired Naval Captain, Capt. McFadden and his wife who added a wing to the customs house in 1957. In 1980, Cdr. Elmer Jackson and his wife, Doris, made some repairs and decorated in the early French Empire style.

Rousby Hall has a huge living room and high ceilings as well as tall windows, a spacious dining room, large kitchen, study and enclosed porch and three large bedrooms. The Kocens bought the property in October of 1987 and have spent five of those years painstakingly restoring the main house, customs house and gardens and making additions. All this work was executed with particular emphasis on authenticity and concern for retaining the original integrity of the property. They decorated in a period reminiscent of the late 1700's, a spartan but comfortable style.

This house is a fine example of Maryland's Maritime Capes', a clapboard waterfront home and working farm similar to those found in the late 18th and early 19th centuries. The Customs House is original.

The grave of John Rousby III is on the 11 acre lawn, and his grave bears the Rousby coat of arms. His widow, Anne, had borne John the daughter, Elizabeth, who married Maryland Governor George Plater and at one time owned Sotterley estate.

When George Plater died, Elizabeth married Edward Lloyd, of Wye House in Talbot County.(5)

This is a private home not open to the public.

Sketch by Don Swann

Mount Airy Plantation

Mount Airy Plantation is a stately residence of landed gentry which has much national historic import (circa 1660). This graceful renovation of Lord Baltimore's hunting lodge redeems Prince George's County's claim as the home of aristocrats in days gone by. Not far from Rt. 301, it is at the Rosaryville turn off down shaded winding roads.

George Washington visited Mount Airy in 1774 to attend the wedding of his stepson John Park Custis to Benedict's daughter, Eleanor. The last of the Calverts to own it were Dr. Cecilius Calvert and his sister Eleanora.

The house has a restaurant in a glassed in addition toward the center, and the library was a lounge/gallery of the Calvert's ancestral portraits. Their dark, brooding eyes seemed to follow one around the room.

Eleanor M. Patterson, publisher of the Washington Times-Herald, completely restored the mansion in the 1930's. It was frequented by many prominent guests, including President Franklin D. Roosevelt and General Douglas MacArthur.(3)

In 1973, the estate of 1017 acres was purchased by the Department of Natural Resources and designated as Rosaryville State Park. It is not presently open to the public.

Anne Arundel

While Spanish explorers arrived inside the Chesapeake Bay in 1566, Southern Anne Arundel County had no settlement in the early 17th century. The first Englishmen to visit this area were Captain Lane in 1585 with an artist, John White, who drew detailed maps of the Bay. In 1608 Cpt. John Smith explored the area.

In April 1672, George Fox, founder of Quakerism, opened the first General Meeting of Friends in Maryland at Rt. 468 and Rt. 255 near the present town of Galesville.

Holly Hill

Holly Hill at 333 Friendship Road near Friendship off Rt. 2   has the distinction of being one of the oldest house in the State of Maryland. The dendrochronology study made in 1982 proved that the earliest part of the house was built in 1698, the earliest date for the houses studied. Brice Clagett, a descendent of the original platter of this property, and his wife Diana live in this T-shaped brick home, which began as a two room wooden house.

By 1730, the house had become a one and one half story brick dwelling. It had been rebuilt within brick walls in 1704 and further enlarged with a new wing to create the T shaped plan about 1730. (as told to me by Brice Clagett)

Of special interest at Holly Hill are early marbleized paneling and several over-mantel paintings from the second quarter of the 18th century, including the earliest-known painting of an American house. This detailed painting of the house and courtyard of Holly Hill are as they existed in 1730. (tour)

The 40 acre gardens contain hundreds of horticultural specimens. The swimming pool is in a formal setting and the rustic pond is at the skyline. The family cemetery is also on the property.

The Harrisons owned the house for years. They were famous Quakers and, no doubt, abolitionists. An underground tunnel, leading from the basement all the way to the water, may have been used to allow the escape of slaves. But this tunnel can no longer be found.

Tulip Hill

Tulip Hill, visited by Washington and one of the foremost examples of architectural genius in America, is on the National Register and is one of our most beautifully preserved colonial homes in the nation.

Overlooking the West River near Galesville, it was built in 1755-62 by the brickmaker and bricklayer, John Deavour, for Samuel Galloway.

Legend has it that Indians and pirates roamed these shores in early days, and a ghost story is attached to the home.

The land was originally patented to Richard Talbot in 1659. Washington dined here twice in September 1771.

Samuel Galloway who had married Ann Chew, died in 1786, willing the house to his eldest son, John. At his death his only child, Mary Maxey, whose husband was Minister to Belgium, inherited. She left Tulip Hill to her daughter, Ann Sarah Hughes, who sold it to Henry M. Murray in 1886 for $100 a month for the rest of her life. She lived to be 100. (Mr. Harrison Murray)

Her son, Maxcy Galloway Hughes, died in the Civil War in Houston, Texas in 1863. Perhaps, it is Maxcy who rides his horse, laughing happily in the night air near his beloved Tulip Hill, glad to be home, if only in spirit.

Henry Murray's Wife, Mary H. (Morris) was a descendant of the builder of the house. Their son, Robert, lived there thirty years before his father sold the house and 50 acres to A. DuPont Parker of Denver Colorado. Robert then moved into the house next door, Poplar Knoll. (Mr. Harrison Murray)

Tulip Hill was designated a National Historic Landmark in 1970.

The house is perfectly balanced on an axis, stretching from the front drive way, which leads to the circular drive, through the central hallway, down past terraces to the lovely West River. A canopy of trees forms a walk past the terraces to the water, through marsh land, replete with waterfowl and deer.

Twin Copper Beeches stand sentinel near the house in purple splendor. They are 400 years old and one was struck by lightening, weakening only a part of it. The area is pervaded by a holiness about these ancient trees. On the ridges beyond them a beautiful garden was created in 1930, and different flowers bloom every season. (Mr. Wayson)

The front of the house is perfectly balanced under a double hip roof, nearly unique in architecture of the period. The brick work is formed into twin crosses at either side of the door. A screened in porch is on the right wing and a carriage entrance is on the left wing's side, leading to the house from the stables.

The land beyond the stables was sold to the Waysons, when they purchased the property in 1992. The property is now 114 acres.

It was originally named for the beautiful Tulip Poplar trees in the front yard. Several trees are 400 years old. (as told to me by Mr. & Mrs. Wayson)

A hall runs the depth of the house with a large double arch dividing it. The front half contains a corner cupboard. The other half contains the staircase, up which one of the Galloways is said to have ridden his horse. The risers are 6 inches with treads 12 inches wide, so that is possible. This is one of the most beautiful and graceful staircases in existence.(4)

The garden door rises to a hood. On the left of the hall are doors to the parlor and library, spacious rooms with beautiful mantels and panelling. A door to the left leads to the last wing and a sitting room with fireplace.(5)

On the right side of the hallway is the door to an office. The dining room may be entered from this room or from the hall.

A widow walk at the top of the house allows one to survey the perfect symmetry of the gardens and terraces to the water. One of the bedrooms, called the purple room, has a delft tile fireplace with scenes of the apostles from the Bible on all sides and under the mantel. Another bedroom features a marble fireplace mantel, sides and floor.

The story of a secret passage to the river seems conceivable, but this passage has never been found. The owners grant the possibility that a tunnel was underground in the gardens but doubt that it went as far as the water.

A private cemetery with black gates marks the grave of the Maxcy Secretary of State who was killed by the blasting of a cannon on board the Princeton on the 28th of February, 1844 at a boat christening he attended with President Tyler in Washington. Samuel Galloway is also buried here as is Ann Sarah Hughes and Anne Chew. Cypress trees, strange to this climate, grow tall here and pervade the atmosphere with shade of the old South. Perhaps other shades are present here also from a time steeped in mystery and enchantment. (as told to me by Mr. Wayson)

Topside Inn

Topside Inn was owned by the Wayson family as far back as 1691, when Capt. Frances Wayson, a ship's captain, owned it. The property was part of Galloway, which the Galesville area was called then and until about 1915.

Morgan M. Wayson, present owner, Sonny Wayson's great grandfather, owned a boarding house and eatery there when the pier in front was used to unload freight and seafood. The other pier, where steamboat Landing Restaurant now stands is where the steamboat, Emma Giles, arrived. The people who frequented the steamboat were often hungry and thirsty and came to the eatery for refreshment and food.

The Galloway area may have included all of the acreage to where Shady Oaks Boat Yard is today, down Muddy Creek Road.

Now, the Topside Inn is once again owned by the Waysons. The remodeled restaurant is open to the public for both dining and lodging.

A lovely wrap-around porch with New Orleans motif of wrought iron scrolls, looks out on the sparkling West River in a panoramic vista from the second floor. Beyond it, seven guest rooms are ready for lodging with antiques in the period of the 19th century. A private lounge for guests and parties has been created on that floor for intimacy.

Plan a special occasion, such as a wedding in the banquet room below. Then, stay overnight and forget the drive home. Breakfast with southern hominy grits, pancakes or egg dishes can be served on the wrap around terrace, where you can enjoy morning breezes and the beautiful view in fair weather.

This is truly an inn for all seasons. Visit when cold winds blow and be seated near the cozy fire. You're sure to enjoy traditional Maryland dishes, such as succulent Crab Cakes or Italian specialties such as Seafood Fettucini and lite fare. Dance to live music Saturday and Sunday as you linger over international coffee and homemade desserts at the Wayson's historic Topside Inn. Call (410)867-1321 for reservations.

London Town

The American London Town was on the banks of the South River in what is now Edgewater. It was a trade center, dispatching vessels all over the world. Today, only one building of this former one hundred acre town remains. Surrounded by woods and gardens is the tavern house that was at this 18th century cross roads of world trade.

The London Town Publik House was built circa 1760 by William Brown, an enterprising cabinet-maker, who was also licensed to run the ferry from London Town to Annapolis. This South River ferry, docking at the foot of Scott Street, was part of the great north-south highway connecting Williamsburg and Philadelphia.(1)

William Brown, owner and operator of the ferry and London Town Publik House, catered to Anne Arundel County's Loyalists. Anthony Stewart, who was forced by colonists to burn his tea-importing brig," The Peggy Stewart", in 1775, retained a room once a year in the Publik House. James Dick, who owned much of London Town, including a mortgage on the Publik House, might have dined here in the privacy of the River Room.(2)

Here was a well run establishment, where the four corner rooms were elevated six inches off the entry passage to block the cold air. In one room, a reproduction poster bed exhibits draperies hanging from a canopy, and three mattresses of corn husks, horse hair and wool cardings.

The date of the construction was set between 1758 and 1764 from Brown's mortgages, and he finally lost the house to his creditors. Its unfinished interior attests to that fact, since being a cabinet maker, he would have finished it in precise detail, if he had had the funds.(3)

Yet, Brown did accomplish a fine amount. He built a comely and enduring Georgian structure, which in 1806, became a tenant house in the estate of Maryland Governor John Stone, a private house for James and Mary Larrimor c. 1828, and later, the Anne Arundel County Almshouse.(4)

The house was reconditioned for use as a county museum in the early 1970's and eight acres of woodland gardens were created, offering an unusual combination of native and exotic plants. A pavilion is now glassed in near the garden shop for indoor weddings, and outdoor weddings are held near the water.

The house's interiors with original cloak and hat boards, doors, hardware and original glass make it a fine example of an 18th century ordinary. The all header brick facade is of brick bond, rare in the nation. A three bay wide central pavilion is surrounded by a pediment with a lunette window. Two huge chimneys form an apex which was a landmark for ships coming to Thomas Point from the Chesapeake Bay.(4)

The house and gardens and Museum & Garden Shop are open Tuesday through Saturday 10 - 4, and Sunday 12 noon - 4 from March 15 - November 15. House tours are given on the hour Call 410-222-1919.

Annapolis

"The appeal to the rights of man, which had been made in the United States, was taken up by France, first of the European nations. From her, the spirit has spread over those of the South. The tyrants of the North have allied indeed against it, but it is irresistible. This is a wonderful instance of great events from small causes."
Thomas Jefferson

Annapolis, our state capital and one time capital of our nation, has more than those claims to fame. This home of the United States Naval Academy also fostered four signers of the Declaration of Independence as long time residents.

The home of Charles Carroll of Carrolton is still being restored. William Paca's home, renowned for its gardens, had a new lease on life, thanks to Historic Annapolis, formed, just as the plans for destruction were in the wind.

Samuel Chase's home on Maryland Avenue is one of the foremost examples of colonial architecture. The Peggy Stewart House near the Naval Academy was the home of signer Thomas Stone from 1784 until his death in 1787. He purchased it from the owner of the ship," Peggy Stewart", burned with its cargo of tea.

These beautiful homes still extant in this little seaport town on the sparkling Chesapeake Bay are historical treasures.

Even local residents often forget that their city ranked in importance with Philadelphia, Boston and New York at the time of the Revolution. Walk the same cobbled streets here that Washington, Jefferson and Franklin strolled.

Many war time decisions were made here in the taverns that still stand.

For several years Annapolis served as temporary Capital of the nation. The city was instrumental in the peace effort long after the decisive fall of Cornwallis in our victory at Yorktown. General Washington resigned his commission before Congress on December 23, 1783 in the new State House building. In Annapolis three years later, Congress ratified the Treaty of Paris, officially ending the war and appointed Thomas Jefferson Minister to Europe. Annapolis was already 135 years old.

Although Annapolis was replaced by Baltimore as the commercial center after the Revolution, the town did not become derelict. It did not have the deep harbor for commerce that Baltimore has, and that fact in itself may have aided its preservation. It was not ravaged by the Civil War and most of the historic structures remained in use and occupied.

During the "Great Depression", the town began to fade into a ghost town. Merchants were trying to give their shops a modern look to preserve trade. Shopping centers became popular in the 1950s and merchants began to propose parking lots in towns and called for demolition of important buildings.

In 1953 a small band of citizens formed the preservation organization now called Historic Annapolis Foundation to restore and preserve old buildings even if they had to be utilized in new ways. Obstacles against their cause were severe.

In the end, the preservationists won out, however, and by 1970, Annapolis was in a glorious renaissance period. Paul Pearson and other historically concerned individuals recreated four historic inns near Church Circle in the center of town. Others took up the cry, and the rebirth of this colonial capital had commenced.

That year, Annapolis was already 115 years old. At this writing, Annapolis is celebrating its 300th anniversary. It is one of the oldest and perhaps the best preserved of American cities. While Williamsburg had to be rebuilt, Annapolis was fortunate in that certain citizens cared enough to save its old buildings and even keep much of their contents in tact.

It has retained its colonial identity because of the preservation of colonial as well as perfect examples of Federal, Victorian, Greek Revival and other period architecture.

Photograph by Marion E. Warren

Middleton Tavern

The famous Middleton Tavern at 2 Dock Street, was frequented by Washington, Jefferson, Franklin and Monroe. The ferry that carried them to and from Philadelphia belonged to Samuel Middleton.

An 18th century tavern served as a communication network, a source of commerce and was important in the social structure. Middleton Tavern hosted the Maryland Jockey Club, Free Masons, and the renowned Tuesday Club, an organization of most erudite gentlemen with well documented records, that provide a glimpse of life in Annapolis 200 years ago.

The tavern's Georgian style building, probably constructed in 1748, was owned by Elizabeth Bennett, who in 1750, sold it to Horatio Middleton. Ferry operators had to have lodging for travelers. Thus, it became an inn.

Samuel Middleton, son of Horatio, is mentioned in the records of the Tuesday Club and in journals of Washington and Jefferson.

One night, the Tuesday Club, took over the tavern, and this verse from local lore was written about Samuel's involvement:
"Middleton frisk's on one leg at such a rate, you'd swear that it stood in no need of its mate."

In 1791, when his ferry transporting Washington ran aground, the Father of our Country spent a night "wedged in a bunk too short by a head", he recorded. (Washington's Journal)

The restaurant was opulent and looked out on formal gardens from Prince George St. to the water. In the 1780's, it was purchased by John Randall, once a partner of William Buckland.

With its stone fireplace, oak panelling and pewter platters, it made a cordial meeting place.

When Jerry Hardesty purchased it in 1968, he was only 26 and had studied the family mortuary business. He preferred to take care of live people, and restored the tavern with close attention to colonial decor, changing the name back to Middleton Tavern

When fires of 1971 and 1973 gutted the building, he restored it twice again, then in 1983, remodeled and expanded to include an oyster bar and banquet facilities upstairs.

Middleton Tavern has many authentic accents. The rack of herbs denotes how herbs were prized as culinary seasonings, for fragrance, beauty and medicine. Fashionable ladies carried a "tussy mussy", a pouch of fragrant herbs to place over their noses on encountering odors. The Shiplap House just up the street has a beautiful herb garden.

The rack of tobacco shows how this leading product of Maryland was cured. It was even used as currency. Visit the Tobacco Prise House closeby.

The Oyster Bar pays tribute to the succulent bivalve and watermen, who, with the ploughman, are on the State's Great Seal. The farm tools in the dining room came from lower Anne Arundel County, original home of the Hardestys.

It is said that no one living in Colonial Annapolis, needed to go hungry, as they could live like kings on the bounties of the Bay and farmland.

The Middleton Tavern pays tribute to Bay treasures in its sumptuous menu items. Enjoy Chateau Briand for two, Crab Middleton, and many Southwestern delights along with the famous Oyster Shooters and Samuel Middleton's Ale. The Hardesty touch of cordiality, creativity and love of authenticity can be observed in every aspect of this inimitable historic tavern.

The resident ghost is a prankster, hiding silverware from servers and adding a bit of mayhem to the merriment in the banquet room. Call 410-263-3323 or 261-2838 for reservations.

Corner Cupboard

The Corner Cupboard at 30 Randall Street is a privately owned bed and breakfast. This home was built circa 1870 in the vernacular style. Conveniently located near the Naval Academy, fine shops and restaurants, it is one of the most accessible and intimate of the Annapolis inns.

The cordial owners, Lise and Vic DeLeon, have recently renovated and decorated their old house in period motifs. To recreate the antique ambiance, the original pine floors have been restored and Oriental carpets are used. Luxurious moire-style wallpapers, antiques and portraits of the times add accents of gentile charm.

A beautiful round table and silver service gleam under the watchful eye of the owner's three greats grandmother from her portrait in the dining room. Her marriage certificate to Moses Palmer, dated 1824, is displayed nearby. Here also is the inn's name sake corner cupboard dating back to 1850.

In the parlor beyond, hangs a tavern sign from the period and a wall of ancestral portraits. A lively Oriental carpet and family antiques lend cheer to this cozy room with its working fireplace.

Looking through this room, we see a dine-in kitchen with a sewing machine, side table and rocking chair with hand painted song birds. This cheerful room looks out onto a lovely city garden, where breakfast is also served in fair weather.

Up the front hall staircase are two fine guest rooms, The "Rose Room", decorated in soothing pink tones, offers a queen bed with half canopy. A love seat and wing chair create an intimate sitting area. The second room, the "Bear's Room", features antique oak furniture. Its massive bed and matching bureau with carved lions heads is distinguished.

Fresh flowers candies and a small basket, toiletries are some of the luxurious touches awaiting your enjoyment.

In the morning, a full breakfast is served in the dining room with a selection of fruit, fresh pastry and a wide choice of entrees.

The house is centrally air conditioned and heated, and you can readily avail yourself of off street parking. Call 410-263-4970 for reservations.

The James Brice House

"Conquest and tyranny, at some early time, dispossessed man of his rights, and he is now recovering them." Thomas Paine

Captain John Brice emigrated to Maryland from Haversham, England. He was a gentleman, merchant-planter and came in 1698. He married Sarah Howard, widow of Maryland Planter, John Worthington, and daughter of Matthew Howard, who purchased Pendennis Mount from Edward Lloyd and Greenbury Forest from Colonel Nicholas Greenbury.(1)

John Brice and Sarah Howard Worthington Brice had three children. Ann who married Vachel Denton, a mayor of Annapolis, and Rachel who married Colonel Phillip Hammond. Rachel and Phillip's son, Matthias Hammond, built the Hammond Harwood House. Captain John Brice's first child by Sarah Howard was John II, a mayor of Annapolis and Chief Justice of Maryland. John II married Sarah Frisby, great granddaughter of Augustine Herrmann of Bohemia Manor in Cecil County.(2)

The James Brice House at 42 East Street in Annapolis was built during the period of 1767 to 1773 by James Brice, later known as "the Colonel". John Brice II left his younger son James, lot ninety four and building materials to erect a dwelling house with outhouses. The building, next to the Paca House, is distinguished by its great size and dignity and huge chimneys.

Designated a National Historic Landmark in 1970, Brice House is an excellent example of Georgian 5-part architecture.

The chimneys rising from the gable ends are 90 feet above the ground, over an elevated basement. The east wing originally contained the kitchen and the west wing, the children's schoolroom, laundry and carriage house.

The entrance hall staircase is constructed from Santo Domingan mahogany, with plain baluster and a molded handrail. Above a running fret are carved rinceau brackets at each riser.(3)

This huge mahogany staircase with carved C scroll stair ends and molded handrail is impressive. The foyer leads into a parlor, often referred to as the ballroom, which is a vivid turquoise blue (as analyzed by electron microscope during the restoration- which told restorationists that the colors were not drab in colonial times) The spacious room has ornate cornices, more detailed than any in Annapolis, and a carved wood mantelpiece with Rococo designs.

The room called the dining room by James Brice was where Washington and Lafayete probably dined with Colonel Brice. It features unusual raised plaster Adamesque paneling and wainscoting which was painted yellow and duplicated the room's original color. It probably contained two mahogany dining tables and a dozen Windsor chairs which he purchased in Philadelphia in 1771.(4.)

James Brice may have also entertained dignitaries in the green room or gentlemen's parlor. Aside from membership in the Governor's Council he was twice Mayor of Annapolis after the Revolution and interim governor of Maryland in 1792. He was married in 1781 at age 34 to Juliana Jenings and they raised five children.

When he died in 1801, his widow inherited the house and lived there with two of her sons. A ghost story concerns the death of one of these sons allegedly at the hands of a manservant. Late one-night, the 80 year old man was hit on the head with a heavy object. He died soon after he was hit. His ghost was later "heard" in the halls of Brice House. He was the last Brice.(4)

In 1873, Thomas E. Martin, Mayor of Annapolis, acquired the property. His descendants sold it for use of the Carvel Hall Hotel in 1911, and in 1927 it was acquired by St. Johns College. In 1953, Mr. & Mrs. Stanley Wohl purchased and meticulously restored the exterior, while also preserving the interior plaster and woodwork.(5)

It was sold at auction to settle the Wohls' estate in 1982 to the International Union of bricklayers and Allied Craftsmen. It is being adapted as headquarters for the masonry industry of the U.S. and Canada. who consider it a monument to their artisanship. The easement of the Historic Foundation is on the entire interior, and it can never by altered.(6) The Foundation opens it to the public 100 days of the year.

The Little Brice House

Ariana Vanderheyden Jennings (1690-1741) was the daughter of Anna Margeretta Herman and Mathias Vanderheyden, and granddaughter of Augustine Herman, and grandmother to John Brice III. Her first husband was James Frisby, by whom she had Sarah, wife of John Brice II. Her second husband was Thomas Bordley; her third, Edmund Jennings, Sr.

Judge Nicholas Brice committed the oral family tradition of her ghostly appearance to writing in 1844 *"A tradition in relation to Ariana Jennings was communicated to me by my father (John Brice III of Annapolis, her Grandson, as handed to him by his Father, who had married her eldest daughter by James Frisby, now more than a hundred years ago.*

That a Miss Turner who lived in his Father's family (and was well acquainted with Mrs. Jennings before she went to England), having occasion to go into the best parlor (as it was then called) to get something out of a closet near the fireplace, saw a female figure, apparently ill with the small-pox with her face tied up, and sitting in an armchair under a full length portrait of Mrs. Jennings that was suspended over the mantlepiece.

She immediately recognized the likeness of that figure to the lady, and believing it to be an apparition, hastily retreated and communicated the matter to John Brice II, my grandfather, who was so struck by Miss Turner's narrative that he took down the day, hour, et.., and circumstances attending this appearance. It is added that the first letters received from England conveyed the intelligence that she had died in April, 1741 of the smallpox, corresponding in every respect with Miss Turner's account of Mrs. Jenning's apparition, even to the hour of her death. – N. Brice 1844

The above apparition appeared in the Little Brice House at 195 Prince George Street, It belonged to Amos Garrett, the first mayor of Annapolis who took office in 1708. In 1737, the house and lot were sold by the Garrett heirs living in London, to John Brice II. (Broad Neck Hundred Journal, Vol. III, No. 2 pg.26)

The William Paca House

"Man acquires a knowledge of his rights by attending justly to his interest, and discovers in the event, that the strength and powers of despotism consist wholly in the fear of resisting it, and that in order 'to be free', it is sufficient that he will it." Thomas Paine

"As for me, give me liberty or give me death" Patrick Henry

The Paca House and Garden at 186 Prince George Street in Annapolis belonged to famous Maryland patriot William Paca. The Philadelphia-educated, Annapolis-trained lawyer commissioned a five-part brick mansion to be built in 1763 for himself and his bride, Mary Ann Chew. It was the first 5 part mansion in the area.(1)

For her, he had a fine garden constructed, with rare flowers, an artificial brook, a bath house and other lovely features. Today, the Paca Garden ranks among the less than six eighteenth century gardens of the period in the nation.

The brick work on the front of the mansion is plain, but the interior is enhanced with a Chinese latticework stairway and overmantel carvings, adapted from English architecture books. (Baltimore Sun Paper, May 23, 1843, October 11, 1843.) Two one story wings are joined to the main portion of the building by passages, Each has a complex architectural history; both wings have undergone extensive alterations during the mansion's two century history.

William Paca lived there from 1765, when the mansion was completed, until he sold it in 1780.

During these years in Annapolis, he served in The House of Delegates, as a representative to the Continental Congress, and as a signer of the Declaration of Independence. He was recognized for his distinguished service in the Revolutionary War, and when the state government was inaugurated, Paca became a senator in the Maryland General Assembly. He later served three terms as Governor of Maryland and was chosen a member of the Maryland convention, which ratified the Constitution of the United States. He was a good friend of Samuel Chase and was also in close contact with George Washington. If the U. S. had not won the Revolutionary War, Paca and all signers would have been shackled, sent to England and hung as traitors.

The interior of the house contains much of the original wood work. The famous drawing room has a handsome chimney piece with a cornice shelf supported on a frieze with oak leaf trim. Scarlet drapes adorn the windows in contrast to the bright aqua walls of this room to the left of the front door.

The room to the right was a less formal family room and the portrait here is of James and Julianna Brice. William Paca's chair is in this room. Many of his possessions were destroyed in a fire in his house on the Eastern Shore in 1879. A picture of Stephen Bordley, to whom he was apprenticed as a lawyer is in this room.

To the left rear of the hall, a dining room looks out on the gardens. It has an elaborate floor cloth and John Paca's portrait is on the wall. (He was their only surviving child.) Hand painted china and candle sticks are donations from the Paca descendants.

Upstairs is John's nursery with cradle, standing stool and picture of "pudding" clothes which protected the baby from falls. A portrait of Samuel Middleton's cross-eyed daughter-in-law hangs in this room. A bedroom displaying the process of cleaning, conducted twice a year is on this floor along with the master bedroom in which Mary Chew entertained women friends, did needlepoint and had teas. She died in 1774, shortly after her 4th childbirth, and Paca sold the house in 1780 to Thomas Jenings, a fellow attorney.

In 1907, a hotel building was attached to the north side, and the complex later became known as the Carvel Hall Hotel, because it was thought to be the setting for a popular romantic novel of that name. The hotel was a center of social activity for state legislators, Annapolis visitors and U.S. Naval academy personnel. At one time Carvel Hall Hotel/Paca House was slated for demolition, but it was restored by Historic Annapolis. During some of these processes, brick masons reported that they found footsteps in the concrete floor of the basement which stopped abruptly and were purported to be the footsteps of a ghost.

When Paca House became Carvel Hall, all of the beautiful garden was destroyed. A Charles Wilson Peale Portrait of William Paca reveals features of the garden in the background. It contained an intricate irrigation system, a free-form pond and a spring house and unusual two story domed summer house with urn shaped finials at each corner. It was lovingly restored by the foundation. The House is open to the public Mon - Fri 10 - 5 and Sat. & Sun 12-5. Call 410-263-5553.

Photograph by Marion E. Warren

The Chase Lloyd House

Chase-Lloyd House, across from Hammond-Harwood, is on the corner of Maryland Avenue and King George Street. This is the only three storey house in Annapolis built before the Revolution. It takes its name from two men who were implemental in that time, though of very different backgrounds.

Samuel Chase was a man of the common people and could not claim great wealth. He did have great legal skill and energy, however, and was a man of big dreams. He served many times on the House of Delegates before President Washington appointed him to the Supreme Court of the U. S. in 1796. (1)

In 1769, Samuel Chase purchased land for the house from Denton Harwood. He had dreamed of building a house similar to that of Charles Carroll of Carrollton. Tied down by financial limitations, however, Chase was unable to fulfill his vision. In 1771, Edward Lloyd IV bought Chase's exterior structure, and exchanged other property with Mathias Hammond to provide suitable enough space for a large house.

Edward Lloyd, called "Edward the Magnificent" because of his wealth and aesthetic taste, finished building the dream house that Samuel Chase had begun. The mansion was exquisitely beautiful and

Edward Lloyd entertained sumptuously in his home. One of his guests was Lafayette. His daughter, Mary, wed Francis Scott Key, composer of the national anthem in 1802.

Lloyd served in the Continental Congress and was a member of the Convention of 1788, which ratified the Constitution. He died in 1796, and ownership of the house went to Colonel Lloyd, his son. Hester Ann Chase, second cousin of Samuel, bought the house in 1846, to return it to the Chase family. At her death in 1875, she willed the mansion to her three nieces, granddaughters of Samuel Chase. The last surviving niece, Hester Ann Chase Ridout, willed the house to a board of trustees with the provision that the property be established as a home for aged and infirm women. In 1886, it was dedicated to this purpose, which it still maintains today.

A pristine white fence surrounds the house and a flight of steps leads to the white front door, opening on a wide palatially columned hallway featuring a splendid stairway, dividing into flights at a landing. In the dining room and parlor the locks are made of silver and doors are lined with mahogany. Ceilings are of swirling stucco. Sculptured mantels of Italian marble grace many rooms and the vast Palladian window on the stairway has a celestial quality.(4)

The walls of the house are eighteen inches thick and are composed of salmon colored brick laid in Flemish bond. Even the inner side of the interior shutters are carved. The facade is unornamented, in the simple spirit of its builder, but the luxurious interior reflects the tendencies of its second owners. The small brick structure to the right was the original kitchen and is now a separate residence. In the rear and on each side of the building is a garden planted with exotic shrubs and flowers.(5)

The Dolls' House

The Dolls' House at 161 Green street is an enchanting bed and breakfast, which lives up to its name. It contains over 200 dolls of varied types and sizes and three doll houses. One doll house in the dining room, visible as one passes through the foyer, was the inspiration for the inn.

Containing beautiful Victorian furniture, the inn's living room offers comfortable love seats and window chairs, window with interior shutters and tiger oak door frames. The china cabinet, sideboard and many other pieces match this beautifully grained wood. A large oak cabinet is replete with dolls. Other dolls sit in prams and a Vienna regulator clock presides over all.

The house is from the era of 1901 and was originally owned by a judge. The kitchen is the oldest room and is being expanded with a sunroom addition, looking out on the lovely garden.

The front porch is in shades of pink for a fanciful beginning to your stay. Its wicker furniture, doll's rocking chair and bunny sculptures beckon guests inside.

Up the front staircase, on the second floor is the Sun Room in front, a cheerful room in yellow and gold hues. A bathroom next door has a charming doll wall paper border, wicker mirror and lace shower curtain. Down the hall is the Victoria room with its pale pink and blue floral accents. Another bath has oil cloth walls in brown with striking white sculptural touches.

Up yet another staircase is the Nutcracker Suite, an entrancing place for children of all ages. Its sitting room offers dolls in trunks, cradles and rocking chairs. Bride dolls, Raggedy Ann and Andy, a carrousel horse table and a lovely English doll house grace the enormous bed room with two double beds and a romantic chaise lounge.

The entire inn has central air conditioning. Its tiger oak woodwork, Georgia pine floors, brass and tile fireplaces and marble vestibule are the epitome of Victoriana.

Decorated in "Victorian Whimsey" with every doll having a story, this inn is a delightful trip back into yesteryear. Call Barbara and John Dugan at 410 626-2028 for reservations, your tickets for the doll trip.

Charles Carroll House

"Revolutions have for their object, a change in the moral condition of governments, and with this change the burden of public taxes will lessen, and civilization will be left to the enjoyment of that abundance of which it is now deprived." Thomas Paine

Recent restoration of the Carroll House on the grounds of St. Mary's Catholic Church off Duke of Glouchester Street commemorates its most famous inhabitant. Charles Carroll of Carrollton was born in the house in 1737 and used it as his principal urban dwelling until 1821. The Carroll House is the only surviving birthplace of a Maryland signer of the Declaration of Independence, one of four signers' homes in the State, and one of only fifteen in the nation.

The property was first settled in the later 1600's as part of Anne Arundel Towne. Dwelling houses, warehouses and Proctor's Tavern (meeting place for the provincial legislature) were located along the shoreline during those early years. Charles Carroll," the Settler", bought various pieces of the property between 1701 and 1716, soon after Annapolis replaced St. Mary's City as Maryland's capital, and the family owned the land until the mid-19th century when it was conveyed to the Redemptorists, a group of Catholic priests, to be used for religious purposes only.

Carroll," the Settler", had emigrated from Ireland via England, escaping religious persecution to take the post of Attorney General of Maryland. Protestants revolted a year later and he was imprisoned but this setback did not affect him financially in the end. By his death in 1720, Carroll owned 47,777 acres in Maryland and more than one quarter of the lots in Annapolis.

Charles Carroll of Annapolis, "the Settler's" son, diversified his inherited holdings by investing in the Baltimore Ironworks, shipping, agriculture and money lending. He constructed the central block of the current Carroll House in 1721, just eleven feet from his father's frame house, then built a passageway between. The house was 2 stories with a gambrel roof. In 1790 he added 2 more stories with a Gabriel roof and East wing.

In 1737, his son, Charles Carroll of Carrolton, had been born. He was educated at all the best schools of France and England and returned to marry his cousin, Molly, in 1768. He built his "little room for my books" with cathedral window and exterior door in 1770 and enlarged it in the 1790's. It has an exterior door, which was well secured, as he used the room for money lending.

Several of his daughters married well and one of his granddaughters married a Viceroy of Ireland.

He served as a member of the Second Continental Congress and played a behind the scenes role in the writing and ratification of the Bill of Rights in 1787 and later served as one of Maryland's first two senators in the United States Congress and as a State Senator.

The property remains one of very few essentially intact 18th century properties in Annapolis. A Federal Tax Assessment of 1798 places greater value on the house than any in the city and described it as "one brick dwelling 100 x 34 ft. with framed addition 52 x 22 ft. with wash house wood house, "poultry house", stable and coach house.

Exterior restoration of the house was completed in 1986. A 400 ft long 18th century stone seawall was found, which had been a retaining wall for the garden's lowest terrace. The garden's plan consisted of five broad, grass covered terraces and four slopes which formed an almost complete right triangle, unique to the city. The waterfront and western ramp lead to the Carroll kitchen door.

The kitchen may have had a brick floor and curved fireplace of brick which was plastered over. What may have been a slave room behind this kitchen had a wood floor with a shallow space underneath. Archaeologists found artifacts scattered densely there. They excavated a small collection of objects including 12 clear quartz crystals, pieces of chipped quartz, a clear faceted glass bead, a polished black stone and an English-made porcelain bowl. Scholars of West African cultures agreed that the objects had been part of an African divination system, based on spirituality and the after-life. In Sierra Leone, glass objects placed below doorways are symbols of ancestral protection.

Charles Carroll of Carrollton did free his slaves later in life.

Ghostly happenings include a telephone that rings on Sunday mornings, but when the Docent answers, no one is there. A security system also goes off often, although no one has triggered it.

One small room was probably used for preparing food, which may have been sent up to the crystal and china room by a dumb waiter. The original staircase to the second floor is being restored and a ledger indicates that it was carpeted in 12-15 yards of Scottish carpeting. Two rooms that look out on Spa Creek were the living and dining rooms, both with chair rails and fireplaces in the Carroll grey trim color. Charles Carroll, the signer, entertained Washington and Lafayette at this Annapolis residence.

A watercolor portrait of Doughoregan Manor, the settler's first home in Howard County, is in the foyer A portrait of Charles Carroll of Annapolis is nearby. Call 410 269-1737 for tours Friday and Sunday 12 -4, Saturday 10-2.

Hammond Harwood

At 19 Maryland Avenue, opposite the Chase House is the Hammond Harwood House, built between 1774 and 1776 for Matthias Hammond, planter and patriot. The architect, William Buckland, designed many other famous Chesapeake houses. In the spring of 1774, Buckland provided the plan of a five part mansion with polygonal-frontal wings. He also introduced to Maryland the fashionable English concept of an elegantly appointed drawing room on the second floor above a dining room of the same size on the first story. This allowed ladies to withdraw with greater privacy and also displayed a beautiful view of several patriots' gardens down to the water.(1)

Mattias Hammond started to build his home, according to tradition, when he decided to marry and determined to make it the best house in town. While the house was under construction, William Buckland died. The house stands as a dedication to his art, studied by architects and historians. The doorway, possible the finest colonial entrance in America, is beneath a large rectangular window above which is a cartouche opening of intricate beauty.

The front facade faces the street, while the rear overlooks the remains of an extensive garden. The brick house is two stories high with a central section and flanking wings, connected to the main building by a one-storey "hyphens".

The interiors are relatively plain, reflecting the new style of neoclassicism.

Rooms are rather small, perfect in design and always symmetrical. The doors, window sills, mantels, wainscoting, panelling and plasterwork are exquisitely made and in impeccable taste. The ballroom, nineteen by twenty-seven feet, on the rear of the second floor, is made up of a game room and bedrooms. Downstairs, the left wing contains the office, and the right houses the kitchen and what were the slaves quarters.

Matthias Hammond died, unmarried, in 1786 and left the property to his nephew, John. Later, John's brother, Philip became the owner. Ninian Pinkney bought the house in 1810 and sold it a year later to chief Justice Jerimiah Townley Chase, who gave it to his daughter, Frances, as a wedding gift upon her marriage to Richard Lockerman. Their eldest daughter wed William Harwood, great grandson of the architect, William Buckland. Of their four children, Hester Ann Harwood survived the others.(4) During hard times, the kitchen fireplace was used for cooking. When the house was being restored, the beautiful mantel was found intact in the attic, where the owners had carefully placed it. Upon Hester's death in 1924, the treasures of the house were dispersed at an auction sale.

In 1926, St. John's College bought the house and planned to restore it as a museum of early Americana. Later, the Hammond-Harwood House association filled it with 18th century furniture and Peale Portraits and opened it to the public.(5.) Call 410-269-1714.

Chez Amis "House of Friends"
85 East Street
Annapolis, Md. 21401
410 263-6631 or (800) 474-6631

Queen Anne's County

"As reforms, or revolutions... extend themselves among nations, those nations will form connections and conventions, and when a few are thus confederated, the progress will be rapid, til despotism and corrupt government be totally expelled [from] Europe and America. Thomas Paine

Although seemingly peaceful, except for the dash of vacationers over the Bay bridge, Kent Island was not always so serene. From its early days, the island was pervaded by a dark and grisly history in which love, betrayal and murder are a part of its tapestry.

The Kent Island history is tied to the fortunes of the "notorious William Claiborne" and his disputes with the Calverts.

He had been in charge of the Kent Island Plantation for 3 years when the Ark and Dove arrived with Leonard Calvert at St. Mary's City. In about 1625, Governor Yeardley of Virginia had issued a licence for Claiborne to "trade and truck with the Indians", and on May 16, 1631, King Charles I issued Caliborne a license to trade in the Chesapeake.

This was more than a year before Cecil Calvert received his charter to the Province of Maryland. Yet, Cecil Calvert instructed his brother, Leonard, to arrest Claiborne if he did not submit "unto his Lordship' patent".(1)

Claiborne had established a trading outpost at Palmer's (now Garrett island), and his man, Cpt Smith, was prepared to guard it from the traders of St. Mary's City. An attack was made on their Maryland pinnace and the St. Mary's Assembly passed an act "censuring Smith for Pyracie".(Ibid.)

The Calverts retaliated by seizing Claiborne's pinnace," Long Tayle," near the mouth of the Patuxent. All this occurred during 1631-1632, before Maryland was ever formed.

In 1634 Capt. Claiborne appealed to Sir John Harvey, Governor of Virginia, to learn what attitude he should assume towards the newcomers of St. Mary's. The governor replied that they "knew no reason why they should surrender up the right of that Place of the Isle of Kent."(Ibid.)

The fued led to bloodshed when the men from St. Mary's began trading with Eastern Shore Indians. Two of Lord Calvert's ships repulsed one of Claiborne's, Three of Claiborne's men and one of Calvert's were killed. Claiborne returned to England, whether of his own accord or at the insistence of his partners. The new commander of the island, George Evelin, accorded with the Calverts but John Butler and Thomas Smith continued the dispute. Calvert arrested several men and captured both Butler and Smith, who was hanged for piracy after a trial which was a travesty, and other Kent Island inhabitants were hung "without any tryall of Law". Ibid. Legend has it that Bloody Point was the scene of these hangings.

It is probable these disputes that are responsible for the fact that "all physical evidence of 17th century life has long since vanished from the island". The oldest houses to survive are all brick, 1-1/2 stories and one room in depth. Stinton or Old Point is the only early house on Kent Island with a known date, 1722, on its gable end.

William Claiborne's personal plantation was at Crayford. The house was fortified and palisaded and known as Crayford fort. After the reduction of the island by Lord Baltimore, the property was used as the headquarters of the Commanders of Kent. A pair of mill stones found on the farm are believed to date to Claiborne's time. Of buildings extant today at Crayford, the earliest is a small, log plank meat house, dating to the latter part of the 18th century.(2)

Kent Manor Inn

The Kent Manor Inn, on the first exit to Rt. 8, is one of the most spectacular historic attractions in Maryland. It rises majestically, just a mile from historic Stevensville and near the site of Maryland's first settlement on Kent Point in 1631.

The inn is on the State Inventory of Historic Places and was named Maryland's top country inn by the readership of Country Inn Newspaper in 1993.

In this gracious antebellum mansion, built c. 1820, one may step back to a time of quiet country elegance. Romantic touches, such as a cupola with love notes on the walls take us back to the times of Scarlet O'Hara. From this glass observatory, one can look down over lush fields to the water beyond over a treasure land of deer and waterfowl, such as Canada

Geese, ducks, doves, Great Blue Herons, and Snowy Egrets.

Stepping through the welcoming front doors into the foyer, you are greeted by a drawing room with marble fireplace on the right and several dining and banquet rooms on the left, graced with Victoriana. Near regal draperies of mauve satin, one may dine on damask linen and lace. Oriental carpets cushion the fine old floors and mounted waterfowl preside over your feast.

At the hallway's end is a glass enclosed veranda in white and green hues, looking out on the Garden House, which is perfect for weddings.

The inn features 24 period guest rooms, each with its own private bath. These luxurious climate controlled rooms, while decorated in the Victorian style, contain comforts far beyond those of the original farmhouse. Yet, it was a model house for its time with a working fireplace in each room, embellished by fine Italian marble. These fireplaces still function today, as the new owner has spared no effort to make your stay a genuine delight. Whether you visit the inn for a business conference or on a pleasure trip, your stay will afford lasting memories.

The site is a historic one, having been part of the tract called Smithfield which comprised "The Courthouse now Wetherell", granted to Thomas Wetherell in 1651, part of Marin's Neck in 1746, Tarkill (a part of Mary's Portion) in 1753.(l), all purchased by Dr. John Smyth and renamed Smithfield and Smith's Neck (A Courthouse existed on Kent as early as 1658 and was evidently on the tract called "The Courthouse now Wetherell", but the site has never been identified.(2)

According to the 1798 Federal tax, Mary Smyth owned 277 acres of Smith's Neck and fields and Sudler's Chance. It stayed in the Smyth family until 1843 (3) when Sarah Smyth, wife of Dr. Samuel Thompson, gave 309 acres in a deed of gift to her son, Alexander. The Thompson heirs sold it to J.B. Bright in 1898. (4) His oldest son opened the house as a summer hotel called "The Brightsworth Inn", which closed in 1911. In 1917, they sold it to the Reifsneiders who sold it to the Cockey family in 1922. It was later opened as a hotel by Theodore Tolson and called Kent Hall. In 1951 the farm was purchased by T.Worth Jamison and named "Pennyworth Farm"(5).

It is the largest surviving Victorian dwelling recorded in the county.(Ibid)

The eastern portion of the house was built c. 1820, the central portion by Alexander Thompson in l828, and the new East wing by the previous owner, Fred Williams. A large parking lot is on the western side.

A sumptuous breakfast buffet from the three star restaurant is included in the reasonable rates. Please call 410-643-5757.

l.Queen Anne's Co. Rent Roll, f. 310 H. 2.

Archives of Maryland, Vol 54,f.152.

3.Deed RT #C f 203, 4.Queen Anne's Co. Rent Roll f. 310 H. 5. Archives of Maryland, Vol. 54, f. 152. 4. Deed JT #6 f. 30.

5. Of History and Houses, Kent Island Heritage Society, Schoch, 59.

The Hermitage

The Hermitage on Tilghman's Neck was the original cradle of the Tilghman family in America. William Tilghman came from Snodland in Kent, England, where their home was "Holloway Court". Dr. Richard Tilghman, a skilled surgeon, was his grandson. He left England at the time when a petition for the execution of King Charles I was being signed, and some say that he was a signer, although his name was not on the petition. He came to America in 1638.

When he first came to America, he bought a tract in Calvert Co. called Canterbury on land which is now off Oxford Rd. In 1659, he purchased the Hermitage, called Cedar Branch, from James Coursey. The original grant was from Cecilius Calvert. The tract covered many times the original grant of 400 acres by the time the Tilghmans had it. Portions were called Waverley, Greenwood, Piney Point, and Oakleigh.

The original house," The Hermitage", burned in 1850 but was rebuilt. Matthew Tilghman,son of the second Richard and a delegate to the Continental Congress, lived there. The lane leading up to the stately edifice is lined with lofty pines. the Tilghman burying ground is near the entrance, under weeping willows. Dr. Richard Tilghman is buried there. A fairly recent owner was Susan Williams, a descendant of the Tilghmans. She remained single but she willed the house to Benjamin Tilghman who lives there still.

The Tilghmans also had another tract of land near Easton called Gross Coate, since it was patented in 1658 to Roger Gross by Lord Baltimore. Located where the Wye River converges with Lloyd Creek, the 250 year old house is a fine example of Georgian architecture and the replica of an English country house. The Tilghmans owned it from 1760 until 1983 when Molly and Johathan Ginn purchased it. They told me a ghost story about the Tilghman's "Aunt Molly" who lived there with her brother, Richard, and family in 1790, when she met the love of her life, Charles Willson Peale, the famous portrait painter. He had been hired to paint portraits of the family and fell in love with Molly. However, when he asked for her hand in marriage, Richard became enraged and demanded that Peale leave, locking Molly in her room.

Legend has it that Molly's subsequent unhappy marriage was her retaliation against Richard's actions. Her life was spent lavishing affection on a favorite nephew, who also had a rebellious streak. When he would stay out late, Molly would let him in the front door. Later Tilghmans said they often saw "Aunt Molly" after she died, attending to her nightly door duties.

Bloomingdale Place

Bloomingdale Place, a Colonial Georgian Manor dating to 1792, has a columned pediment on both storeys divided by a terrace on the top storey. From the entrance, a long hall leads to a spacious living room on the left and dining room on the right. Descendant of the original owners live in the house and open it to parties for wedding and reunions inside or out with outside catering. This is not a bed & breakfast or inn. It may be viewed from Rt. 50 near Queenstown and may be reached by Bloomingdale Road off Rt. 301.

Bloomingdale was patented by Captain Robert Morris, under the name of Mt. Hill in 1665. It was acquired by John Seth, who willed it to his son, Charles, who became owner of the entire grant. Later, Thomas Seth acquired the property and sold it to Dr. Edward Harris. He willed it to his daughters, who rechristened the lovely manor house Bloomingdale.

In 1879, Mrs. De Coursey was being entertained by Sallie Harris, one of the doctor's daughters, when they saw a wraith-like spirit ascend the stairway toward the bedroom that Sallie's nephew, William Sterrett, had occupied when he lived in the house before he drowned in the old mill. The spirit entered the bedroom much to the dismay of the shocked women. When Sallie Harris summoned the courage to enter the bedroom, the spirit was no longer there, but the bed clothes were rumpled.

Elegant country weddings are now held in the lower rooms and on the grounds. – (Colonial Families and their Descendants, Queen Annes Homemakers, 1938.)

Chester River Inn Recipes

Curried Zucchini with Crab Soup (serves 12)
INGRIDENTS:
1 qt. chicken broth
1 lb. crabmeat (jumbo lump)
1 qt. heavy cream
1 lemon
1 leek (diced)
2 T. fresh garlic
2 carrots peeled and diced
1-1/2 T. curry
2 stalks of celery (diced)
1/2 tsp. cayenne pepper
4 zucchini (diced)
1 tsp. coriander
2 onions (peeled and diced)
sale and pepper
2 c. julienne carrots
2 cups julienne zucchini
METHOD:
In a medium crockpot, add together chicken stock, diced vegetables and all spices. Bring to a boil. Reduce heat and let simmer until vegetables are tender, about 1-1/2 hours. Remove from heat, place in blender and puree.
Return to stove, add heavy cream and bring to a boil. Add lemon, salt and pepper to taste. Add crabmeat and julienne vegetables. Simmer for three minutes, and serve.

Smoked Salmon with wild rice, leek & corn waffles (serves 16)
INGREDIENTS
2-3/4 smoked salmon (sliced thinnly)
8 oz. cream fraiche
4 T. nonpariel capers (briefly deep fried in peanut oil)
16 oz. fresh horseradish
8 round waffles cut into quarters
16 sprigs fresh dill or fennel tops for garnish

Wild rice and leek and corn waffles
4-1/2 c. water
1-1/2 c. cornmeal
6 Oz. melted butter (unsalted)
3 tsp. peanut oil
3/4 c. corn flour
1-1/2 tsp. baking powder
2 egg yolks
1 c. plus 2 T. milk
3 egg whites
2 tsp. salt
6 oz. cooked wild rice
6 T. finely diced leek (fron the white)
METHOD:
Cook the cornmeal in the water for 5 minutes, then place in a food processor with the butter, oil, corn flour, baking powder, egg yolks and milk. Whip egg whites until stiff and fold with the wild rice, leeks and salt into the corn flour batter. When waffle iron is hot, oil lightly, pour enough batter to cover iron and cook until golden brown. Waffles may be kept for a short time in a 275 degree oven.
Wrap slices of smoked salmon into 16 rosettes. For each plate, place a salmon rosette on a bed of horseradish (approx 2 T.) Sauce the plate with cream fraiche in a zig-zag pattern and sprinkle with fried capers. Set 2 quarters of waffle next to salmon rosette and garnish with dill or fennel.

Colonial Homes of the Eastern Shore

Géddes Piper House

Kent, Talbot, Dorchester & Somerset Counties

Glassgow

Trumpington

Hichingham

Wye House

Wide Hall

Teakle Mansion

Plimhimmon

Photograph by Marion E. Warren

Inn at Pirates Cove

The Inn at Pirate's Cove, that splendid yet cozy old restaurant on the beautiful West River, is in historic Galesville, just twenty minutes from Annapolis. A restaurant has been at that location for more than half a century. Boats have been docking at its door for most of that time, loaded with patrons.

Zang's Pier, a popular restaurant that opened in the 1920's, was located where Pirates Cove Inn is now. Delbert Zang, son of the owners, Capt. Louie and Miss Daisy, tells that Zang's Pier was actually an oyster house with a store above it. When Delbert's father bought it, he turned the oyster house into a restaurant. A bar in front had a wood floor, but the restaurant's floor was concrete, from the oyster days. In the summers, people came from Washington to their summer places around the West River and the Showboat would come to Galesville for a week every summer. It was named after its owner James Adams, and everyone enjoyed the theater there. Part of the building on the left of the Pirates Cove complex is an original building, used as a shed and upstairs was a carpenter shop, now converted into four nice motel units. If you stay overnight at Pirates Cove after a wedding, perhaps, you'll be in the original portion.

The new Big Mary's Dock Bar is also near the original portion, especially the inside cafe with its large peacock chairs and bar. The two large dining rooms of the present restaurant with their tall windows, looking out on the water occupy the original parking lot which was made from just a shell road.

In the late 40's, the Zangs sold Zang's pier to Nelson Smith who later sold it to Dick and Dorothy Renault, who named it Pirate's Cove.

The state archives mention information that a local pirate named Richard Clark ravaged the South River area during the early 1700's, indulged in coun-

terfeiting Spanish pieces of eight and even threatened to burn Annapolis. His accomplices were captured, trying to anchor the sloop, "Margarett's Industry", off Beard Creek to collect Clark's belongings, but the pirate had fled to Virginia and was never seen again by authorities. (*Pirates on the Chesapeake,* Donald Shonette, Tidewater Publishing, 1985.-State Archives.)

The early 80's brought a new owner and a new face lift to Pirate's Cove. Bob Platt, drawing on years of experience, renovated the restaurant from the foyer to the new, appealing waterfront lounge in the rear. His friend, Tom Woodward, a local, well known commercial artist, added life with murals, depicting clam fishermen and tropical scenes for a finishing touch.

Add all this to three large stone fireplaces, rough hewn beams, a beautiful waterfront view, leisure walks on the pier and friendly bar tender Joe Williams with 32 years at the cove, and you have the place folks look for but seldom find. Did we forget to mention the complete menu and tried and trusted recipes?

Oyster lovers enjoy much variety from the raw bar. Try the Cove Oysters, Clams Casino, spiced shrimp and many monthly specials. Flounder Longhorn, a favorite, is a baked filet stuffed with crab imperial and jumbo shrimp. Enjoy Roast Prime Rib of Beef or Chicken Del Mar. Every entree at Pirate's Cove comes with abundant freshly baked bread, warm moist nut bread and crisp tossed salad and, of course, local fresh vegetables. The grand finale might be an international coffee with homemade pie, cake or other confection from pastry chef, Anne. These delights will give you ideas for your next special occasion at the entrancing and historic Pirate's Cove. Call 410-867-2300, DC 261-5050 Balt 410-269-1345.

Pirate's Cove's Oyster Pan Roast

INGREDIENTS:

2 T. butter	1/4 c. oyster liquid
8 oysters	1/2 c. heavy cream
1 T. Chili sauce	dash celery salt
1 tsp. Worcheshire ssauce	T. cayenne pepper
1 tsp. white wine	T. white pepper

METHOD:
Saute oysters in 2 T. butter 2 minutes. Add next 5 ingredients and heat 2 minutes. season and serve on toast points in a bowl.

Photograph by Marion E. Warren

Penwick House

Penwick House continues its tradition of serving excellent fare in an atmosphere of gracious cordiality. A new menu and several other new plans give an exciting lift to the historic home of renowned hospitality.

Audrey Davenport the late owner, herself wrote:

The warmth of the fireplace,

A steaming mug of Wassail,

The romance of candlelight,

A sumptuous meal to please the palate.

When you step through the welcoming doors of Penwick House at Ferry Landing Road and Route 4 in Dunkirk, you do, indeed, enter an enchanting world of Victoriana only 35 miles from Capital Hill. Comforting aromas evoke a sense of returning to grandmother's house and fresh faced servers are symbolic of the Penwick spirit of hospitality. Their frilled caps and aproned calico dresses take you back to another time, another place in the sunlight filled enclosed patio, overlooking the gardens.

And oh, the beauty of the gardens in springtime! This is a perfect place for a wedding reception when daffodils and azaleas are in full blossom. Having sampled the pleasures of the short trip in the unspoiled Calvert countryside, you and your guests may stroll down a brick path, arched over by majestic Paper Mullberry trees that set the stage for the graciousness to follow:

Originally the home of Dr. Thomas Chaney, who built it in 1869, the stately house was discovered by Jim and Audrey Davenport in 1950. They restored it to its former beauty with Audrey's finesse as an interior designer and opened the restaurant, naming it after their three daughters: Penny, Wendy and Vikki.

Robust soups made from Penwick's own stockpot and appetizers such as Escargot Sautee and Swaddled Scallops and the regional specialty, Hot Crab Dip are specialties of Chef Andrew McGinley. Favorite entrees include Imperial Crab Strudel, Roast Rack of Lamb, Seared Duck Breast, Grouper Bastion, Salmon Au Poivre, Veal Anisette. and Shrimp and Scallops Coguille... just to name a few. Many guests choose to enjoy their espresso, cappucinio or latti under the umbrellas outside on the patio surrounded by gardens.

Lunch features appetizers, delightful salads, sandwiches and entrees.

Reserve early for holiday parties or wedding receptions by calling 301-855-5388 or 410-257-7077. Luncheon is served Tuesday thru Saturday from 11:30-2:00. Dinner is served from 5:00p.m.-9:00 Tuesday thru Friday and until 9:30 on Saturday. Sunday Brunch Buffet is served from 10:30a.m.-2p.m. Sunday dinner is served from 4:00 - 8:00p.m. The Penwick House is happy to tailor packages to suit your party needs!

Photograph by Marion E. Warren

Coggeshall House

Just across the way from Paca House at 198 King George Street is Coggeshall House with a spectacular view of the United states Naval Academy Chapel over beautifully landscaped gardens. The retaining brick walls and bluestone terrace hold a colorful array of annuals and perenials.

Coggeshall House, c. 1887, is a meticulously renovated house, which offers spacious rooms, high ceilings, many fireplaces and antique furnishing. This prime location affords privacy in a quiet environment with natural wildlife and birdlife, yet assures one of all the amenities and conveniences of living in the Historic District.

Coggeshall House is adjacent to the Naval Academy and is just blocks from many well known Annapolis attractions, such as its 18th century masterpieces of architecture, waterfront, sailing legacy, historical State House, famous restaurants and charming shops.

Owned and recently restored with great attention to detail by Dr. William and Ruth Anderson Coggeshall, it was named for the first President of the colony of Rhode Island from whom Dr. Coggeshall is directly descended. John Coggeshall arrived from England in Boston in 1632, but was expelled with others for his Quaker tolerance. Built in 1887, the house belonged until 1987, to one family of teachers and civic leaders. A stable was behind the house, as was typical of many homes of this time period.

When the Coggeshalls purchased the house, they completely rewired and replumbed it. Fine German siding was revealed when asbestos shingles were removed from the exterior of the house. A new addition was added to the original house including a modern, spacious kitchen and pantry with dark forest green walls and pristine white cabinets.

Guests are greeted in Coggeshall House as they enter the large front hall with a view of the graceful staircase. The handsome knewl post is original with its retooled handrail and spindles winding up to the third floor suite.

The second floor has a large hallway which curves beneath a skylight toward a sumptuous library with a slate fireplace and beautiful view of the Naval Academy chapel. A tastefully decorated private bedroom and bath are at the opposite end of the hall.

The millwork in the house was milled on site, including the 250 year old Georgia yellow pine which is the flooring in the kitchen, complementing its dark forest green walls and white cabinets.

A full course breakfast is served to guests in the dining room with a fireplace. When weather permits, guests pass through the living room out upon the terraced gardens beyond for breakfast. Dr. and Mrs. Coggeshall welcome guests from around the world to their gracious home. The cordial atmosphere, tasteful aesthetic charm and warmth of the Coggeshalls lure guests to this remarkably beautiful bed and breakfast inn. Call 410-263-5068 for reservations.

Photograph by Marion E. Warren

Photograph by Marion E. Warren

Jonas Green House

"Take Courage, Mortal! Death cannot banish thee from the universe. Benjamin Franklin.

"Men are conservatives after dinner.... They are radicals when their consciences are aroused, and when they hear music or poetry." Emerson.

The history of the Jonas Green House at 124 Charles street is remarkable in several respects. It is a testimony to the ingenuity of a woman and her acceptance in the business life of colonial times. It is a chronicle of the life of a working family of the 4th estate through the harrowing times of the Revolutionary War, The War of 1812 and the War Between the States. The house, itself, is extraordinary because it has been preserved, except for some replastering, just as it was in those days in every authentic detail.

One of the oldest houses in Annapolis, it was named for Jonas Green, a printer to the colony and publisher of the Maryland Gazette, the forerunner of the still published, Capital Newspaper. He, and eventually his widow, sons, and grandson printed the newspaper here. He was also the licensed printer to the Maryland Colonial Legislature, and even printed colonial American currency. He lived in the house from May 1738 until his death in 1767, and the house has been in the Green family ever since. One of the current owners, Randy Brown, is Jonas' five greats grandson. He and his knowledgeable and vivacious wife, Dede, welcome guests to a bed and breakfast here.

Jonas Green had learned his trade in Philadelphia from his cousin, Benjamin Franklin, with whom his wife also worked. He moved to Annapolis to replace a departed printer and to publish the Maryland Gazette. Jonas started his life in Annapolis with his new Dutch bride, Anne Catherine Hoof.

As the years went by, they had fourteen children, many of whom died, and the house grew. When one of the children died of small pox, the readers would not touch the paper, and Jonas had to publish a notice, stating that the paper was published in a print shop in the back yard of the house, and none of the materials used in printing it were exposed inside the house.

Jonas continued as the legislature's printer until his death in 1767. Prior to his death, Anne Catherine, along with producing children and running the household, contributed to the family income by making chocolates to sell on the city dock. She had also worked beside her husband in the printshop. When he died, she immediately took over the paper and printing business with no break in service. She petitioned the legislature to continue their contract with her and received an affirmative reply. As editor and publisher of the Maryland Gazette, Ann Catherine continued her husband's even-handed approach to printing both sides of questions until 1773, when she placed her paper firmly in the patriot camp, becoming what R.L. Demeter calls "midwife to the birth of an aroused american political consciousness". (R.L. Demeter. *Primers, Presses and Composing Sticks.* Women Printers of the Colonial Period, Hicksville, N.Y. Exposition Press, 1979, pg. 97).

She collect debts better than her "hail fellow well met" husband had, and her hard-won prosperity enabled her to actually purchase the house in 1770. After renting it for 32 years, she now owned this house, reminiscent of her native country.

The house has apparently housed Green family members continuously since 1738, although it was owned by George Wells, Frederick Green's son-in-law, from 1845-1877, when ownership passed to the Greens again.

It is a two storey, gambrel roofed structure with two chimneys at each end of brick and frame construction. Today's sidewalk runs along the front of the house and was recently restored by Dede and Randy Brown. The front porch was added sometime in the early 1900's.

Walking with the Browns through the house and through history, you find that most of the wainscoting, fireplace and door surrounds as well as floors are original. The front hall was built in the 1720's and contains original wooden pegs on the wall. In the 1700's, they would have held Master Green's coat and Mistress Green's shawl, and would also have held a fire bucket, as at present.

The hall floor is heart of yellow pine, probably original. a faux grained door (probably done in the early 19th century) is at the end of the hall. A Charles Wilson Peale portrait of Anne Saunders Green hung in the house for many generations, until it was sold out of the family.

The family living room is a lovely, large, sunny room with wide plank floor, built in the 1760's. A fireplace is opposite the door and there are two narrow doors flanking the wooden wainscoting around the fireplace. These are two old gun closets which now contain floor to ceiling bookshelves. The closets have windows, which used to open on a pastoral scene, but now reveal the house next door. This house was built for Harriet Oldham Green's son by his mother, with the proviso that he live there for the rest of his life, which he did.

The closet to the left of the fireplace has a trap door in the floor and narrow, steep stairs that lead to a small basement furnace room.

Across the hall from the family living room is the front parlor, built in the 1740's and used for formal entertaining. This was also where family members were laid out at their deaths.

One portrait in the room is of Harriet Oldham Green who married Dr. Richard Harwood Green, three greats grandson of Jonas. Recently added to this room is a James Peale portrait of William Saunders Green, grandson of Jonas. William was a doctor, who lived in the house from his birth in 1778 until at least 1845 and possible to his death in 1847. He married into the Harwood family which occupied the Hammond Harwood House, still standing on Maryland Avenue. His son, Nicholas Harwood Green's portrait also hangs in this room. He, like his father married into the Harwood family. Of the possible eight grandparents between his bride and him, six were common to both families.

The middle portrait on the street wall is of Eleanor Green Brown (four greats granddaughter of Jonas), Randy's mother. The portrait of her husband, Admiral Brown, is on the back wall. Although Eleanor bought the house from her cousins in 1959, and owned it until her death 28 years later, she never lived here.

After the purchase, the house was rented until 1961, and then stood empty and neglected for 30 years.

At first, Admiral and Mrs Brown, on their retirement after many years in Europe, intended to renovate and move into the house in 1966. They were on their way to Annapolis when the Admiral suffered a massive stroke, necessitating their spending the rest of their lives in Washington near the Naval Hospital in Bethesda.

They had many plans and antiques for the house, but the plans had included many changes. Their son, Randy, and energetic wife, Dede, saw to it that the house was restored from 1991-1992 to keep its origins intact as much as possible.

All of the original structure and house fabric were retained in their original state. In addition, with the help of the Historic Annapolis Foundation, a paint chip study was conducted throughout the house, and the original colors were restored to each room. They also made some interesting discoveries during the renovation.

A ledger, accounting for pay, allowances and purchases for the Prince William County (Virginia) Minute Men, dated 1775 and 1776, was found in the walls. Also, a sort of time capsule on scraps of wood was found between the kitchen ceiling and the floor above. One board contains the inscription: "Richard H. Green, born in this house 1834, this is 1890."

Another, written by a laborer with the heart of a poet, says, "In the year of 1890, John Rnadle and Albert Gaithe, printus boy, done this work for Dr. Green. When this is found, we both will labor in our graves. God luck to all, Good Bye."

Yet another says, "Mandie is the cook at Dr. Green's. She is a good one. 1890." (A Descriptive History of a House and its Family, Mary Donya Brown, Graduate Thesis 1989)

The work the Browns have done on the Jonas Green House has continued a brilliant family tradition and has preserved a treasure of State and National History. May they long be remembered for their work as well. Please call them at 410-263-5892 for reservations.

Photograph by Marion E. Warren

Photograph by Marion E. Warren

Inns and Colonial Homes of Historic Maryland

Photograph by Marion E. Warren

The Chester River Inn

The Chester River Inn, one of the oldest and tallest structures on Kent Island, may be found by turning at the second exit after the Bay Bridge, turning left on the overpass and right to Tackle Circle Road. On the lovely Chester River, it is the domain of famous Chef Mark Henry and his vivacious wife and hostess from Baltimore's Milton Inn.

A peaceful, yet mischievous ghost named Sara is reputed to reside in the lower level, now used as a lite fare pub and for entertainment. The Henry's have not seen Sara, but a cleaning woman who spoke no English, was surprised by Sara one day while in the employ of the former owners. She quit immediately. Silverware is often "misplaced" in Sara's Place. The inn's history reflects the fact that a Sarah owned it at one time.

Built by the Tolson family circa 1857-1860, the property was once called Body's Neck since William Body was granted 100 acres of land in 1650 "for transporting himself in 1649" and 100 more were assigned to him by Robert Dunn. (Isle of Kent Co. Rent Roll, Calvert Papers #880 10 H of R) The whole tract was escheated to His Lordship and granted to John Hynson of Kent County in 1698. It became the right of Sarah Blangy Price, daughter of Jacob Blangy. The Blangy heirs sold it in 1762.

In the unfinished attic, on a rafter is a painted decoration of flowers and a bird, signed: "J.C. Tolson Aug. 4, 1860". This is probably the date of construction.(1)

Today all physical evidence of 17th century life has long since vanished, [from Kent Island], possibly because of the feuds between the Calverts and William Claiborne who had been granted a trading post.(2)

Thus it does not stretch the imagination too much, to surmise that a building, owned by Sarah might have been there in the early 1700's. In any case, the restaurant is in capable hands with the Henrys, and Sara only adds a note of interest to the fabulous fare and noteworthy entertainment offered here.

Fireplaces are in each room, including the basement, probably the original location of the kitchen. Now food is carried down from the kitchen on the second floor near the spacious dining room, looking out on a deck over the water where guests dine al fresco in fair weather.

Summertime appetizers might include Curried Zucchini and Crab Soup, Chilled Shellfish Terrine, Grilled Breast of Duck with bourbon mustard glaze on puff pastry or Ducktrap River Smoked Salmon with creamed horseradish. Some innovative salads might be Smoked Quail with potato, onion and tomato, Chilled Asparagus with mango vinaigrette or Spinach, strawberry, spiced pecans and shaved cheddar. You might enjoy such reasonably priced entrees as Grilled Salmon with roasted pepper and mushroom cous cous, Sesame Scallops with angel hair pasta or Medallions of Chicken & Shrimp with tomato vodka cream on penne. All are in the $17.00 range as is the Roast Loin of Pork with sauteed apples and grit cakes. Baked Swordfish may be filled with four de Latte Mozzarella and crabmeat and Grilled tenderloin of Beef served with tarragon green peppercorn butter. The grilled Chop of Veal is sumptuous with fine Madiera sauce and the Seared Medallions of lamb with rosemary garlic sauce.

Try to save room for the chef's confections such as flourless chocolate cake with cherries and whipped cream. A light meringue with lemon curd and berries is refreshing, while Butterscotch Pudding with real scotch is heart warming on a winter's eve.

Whatever the selection, the Chester River Inn will please the most discriminating connoisseur who demands historic ambience and the finest cuisine. Call 410-643-3886.

Oxford Inn

Presiding with stately grace at the entrance of the historic area of Oxford, the Oxford Inn is a landmark for this quaint village in charming Talbot County.

The American Revolution marked the end of Oxford's early glory. Gone were the British ships with their imported goods. Then, after the Civil War, Oxford emerged from a long slumber of over 100 years. Prosperity came again with the emergence of the rail road in 1887 and improved methods of canning oysters. Business was booming and tourists were arriving in droves.

It was about the time of the turn-of-the-century that the Oxford Inn was built by F.A. Delahaney Overery. The restaurant portion of the inn, called Pope's Tavern, came along when Harry Pope started a waterman's bar there in 1930, which was well known until the 1970's. In the 80's the inn was owned by a couple from Wales who served meals and took in the occasional weary traveler.

Still, it was not until 1989 that the inn received a complete renovation, which the quaint and classic town of Oxford richly deserves. Owners, Rick and Sue Schmitt, completely renovated the two floors upstairs to make 8 lovely guest rooms and suites which have private baths. Three rooms share baths.

The Schmitts literally raised the roof to create the third floor rooms, the Dogwood, Dresden and Stuart Hall, Talisman, Swarthmore, Tavern Hall and Waverly. Each has a different decor and beautiful genuine antiques and period accessories from the turn of the century. Handmade quilts and stained glass accents may be found throughout the inn as well as nautical artifacts.

The boat to the left of the entrance's stained glass doors is called a Log Canoe, one of the first boats in America. The design was borrowed from native Americans and the boards that stick out on the starboard side can be moved to port when the boat leans a different way. The boat above the coat rack is a working boat called a Drake Tail, some of which you can see in port across the road.

The dining room to the left of the foyer has an original fireplace and makes a fine private room for banquets and other parties. The one to the right has a cozy wood burning stove and raw bar under an authentic punched tin ceiling.

Owners Rick and Sue are always gracious and want you to feel completely at ease and pampered as you step back to an era when hospitality was a matter of friendship and good humor in comfortable surroundings. Call 410-226-5220 for reservations.

Bishop's House

The Bishop's House, at 214 Goldsborough Street in Easton, is a Victorian home built by Captain Edward Roberts, a shipwright, for the Honorable Phillp Frances Thomas and his wife Clintonia Wright May Thomas. The Hon. Philip Frances Thomas was Governor of Maryland from 1848 to 1851.

Upon his death in 1892, the house was sold to the Episcopal Church. The house served as the residence of the Bishop of the Diocese of Easton for more than 50 years and is known as The Bishop's House. This name was used in identifying the house at the formation of the Historic District.

John Ippolito and Diane Laird-Ippolito purchased The Bishop's House in 1986, and after two years of extensive and loving restoration work, it has been restored to its former glory. John and Diane opened the house as an owner occupied bed & breakfast to allow others to share the ambiance of their Victorian home.

The Bishop's House is romantically furnished in

period style. The three and 1/2 story home has clapboard walls a gabled roof and includes three spacious first floor rooms with 14 foot ceilings, plaster ceiling molding and medallions. The spacious second floor guest rooms have 12 foot ceilings and working fireplaces. A rectangular oriel window on the second floor compliments the three sided bay window on the first floor below. Ornamental pierced woodwork highlights both the oriel and bay windows. The Bishop's House has a wraparound porch with a standing seam tin roof carried by double square columns.

The focal point of the front drawing room is an exquisite salmon and cream colored faux marbled fireplace. The fireplace in the large dining room has been faux finished in blue and aquamarine.

The main drawing room fireplace has been tiled using Victorian reproductions tiles imported from England. Both the front and main drawing rooms have plaster molding and ceiling medallions.

The Bishop's House has been decorated with intriguing antiques, (including a carousel horse), a fascinating collection of hats, (many contributed by former guests), and historic prints of old Easton and antique pictures.

The Bishop's House is conveniently located in the heart of Easton's Historic District. It is within three blocks of the Talbot County Court House, boutiques, antique shops and fine restaurants which characterizes Easton's main shopping district. Centrally located within 10 miles of historic Oxford and St. Michaels, The Bishop's House provides an excellent location for visiting all points of interest in Talbot County. P.O. Box 2217, 214 Goldsborough St., Easton, MD 21601. Call 1-800-223-7290 or 410-820-7290 for reservations.

The Robert Morris Inn

"In every stage of these oppressions, we have petitioned for redress in the most humble terms: our repeated petitions have been answered only by repeated injuries. A prince whose character is thus marked by every act which may define a tyrant is unfit to be the ruler of a people who mean to be free." Thomas Jefferson

Located on the beautiful strand in Oxford, The Robert Morris Inn is a tribute to the architectural beauty of the 18th century and to its name sake, Robert Morris, Sr., who moved from England to Oxford in 1738. It was built prior to 1710 by ships' carpenters with wooden pegged paneling, ships' nails and hand hewn beams. In 1730, an English trading company bought the house for Robert Morris, who represented the firm's shipping business interests in Oxford.

He achieved a considerable reputation. His son, Robert, Jr., joined him in 1747 at age 13 and lived in Oxford before being apprenticed to a mercantile firm in Philadelphia. Robert Morris, Sr. died in 1750. While he was wading from ship's guns, being fired in his honor, a cannon ball struck his arm.

At the outbreak of the American Revolution, Robert Morris, Jr. was made a partner in the Philadelphia firm. When few would risk money on the new concept of the United States, he used his entire savings to help finance the Continental Army and became a close friend of George Washington, who depended on him to direct the financing of the war.

Robert Morris, Jr. is known primarily by his title, "The Financier of the American Revolution", a reference both to his position as Superintendent of Finance of the United states from 1781 - 1784 and to his role in raising money and supplies for the Continental Government. He was one of only two Founding Fathers to sign all three fundamental testaments of the American Revolution: The Declaration of Independence, The Articles of Confederation, and the United states Constitution. In the line of succession that includes Alexander Hamilton and Albert Gallatin, Morris may be considered the first of the three great Treasury Secretaries who laid the financial foundations of the United States.

The Inn has been enlarged several times since its first use as a private home. The staircase which leads to the guest rooms is the enclosed type of the Elizabethan period and was built prior to 1715. The original flooring in the upstairs hall is Georgia white pine. The nails were hand made, and the 14 inch square beams and pilasters were fastened with hand hewn oak pegs. Four of the guest rooms have hand made wall paneling, and the fireplaces were built of brick, made in England and used as ballast in the early sailing days.

The impressive murals in the dining room were made from wallpaper samples used by salesmen over 140 years ago. The Four Seasons panels: The Plains of West Point, Winnepeg Indian Village, Natural Bridge of Virginia and Boston Harbor were printed on a screw-type press, using 1600 woodcut blocks, carved from orangewood. The murals were painted by an unknown French artist.

In 1962, during the redecoration of the White House, Mrs. John F. Kennedy found the original wallpaper of this design in a historic home in Western Maryland, had the paper removed and placed on the walls of the White House reception room.

The Tavern's slate floor came from Vermont, and over the fireplace is the Morris coat of arms, a magnificent oak, deep relief, carved by John White. The chimney was inspired by the Raleigh Tavern in Colonial Williamsburg. It rises from the massive fireplace in the taproom. Complementing the fine woodwork of this room is a hand carved log canoe under sail, by Ted Hanks of Oxford.

John Moll, the famous Oxford artist, provided the three framed murals adorning the reception hall.

The Riverview room, off the reception hall, has 280 year old pegged wall panels and a fireplace of bricks made in England, circa 1812.

The northern-most three story portion of the Inn, the home of Robert Morris, was 65 years old at the time of the Revolution, and its restoration was designed to recapture the rich heritage of early America.

The Inn has been used as a private residence, a town hall, a boarding house, a temporary convalescence home for WWI veterans, and a general store. In the late 1940's it began to operate as a country inn.

The Inn has established a reputation for consistently serving good food with excellent service. It has been featured in *Country Inns and Backroads,Classic Country Inns of America, Very Special Places and America's Historic Inns and Taverns.*

Unsolicited recommendations have appeared in *Diversion, Southern Living, Washingtonian, Good Housekeeping, Wall Street Journal, Town and Coun-*

try, Better Homes and Gardens, Southern Accents, Discerning Traveler, and *Bon Appetite.* For many years, the Inn has received Travel Holiday's recommended Fine Dining Award. The Inn is dedicated to continuing the tradition of quality which might have been the pride of Robert Morris, Sr. and Jr.

The Oxford Belevue ferry, one of the oldest, makes trips to the Robert Morris Inn from Belevue, near St. Michaels. Call 410-226-5111 for dinner or lodging reservations.

Photograph by Marion E. Warren

Kemp House Inn

The Kemp House Inn, on the main street of St. Michaels, dates back to 1807 and has been restored to be true to those times in every detail. Colonel Joseph Kemp set its foundation after he fought in the Revolutionary War and returned to St. Michaels to become a shipwright. After he built the fine Georgian house came the War of 1812, and he served as a colonel in the militia, which successfully defended St. Michaels. The house remained in the Kemp family for many years and was visited by Robert E. Lee. It continued as a private residence until the 1940's.

Each room, in a different style is furnished in period motif. All have beautiful patchwork quilts on the rope beds and offer old-fashioned flannel nightshirts. Most of the rooms feature working fireplaces, lighted at night. Many have private baths and old fashioned wash stands enhancing the quaint charm.

Firelight, four poster beds and candlelight make it a favorite of honeymooners. Electric lights and air conditioning are also available. Down pillows, wing back chairs and Queen Anne tables grace every room.

One of the few large Federal period brick structures in town, the inn is impeccably crafted with carved mantels, center hall staircase, chair rails, beaded baseboards and heavy pegged and paneled doors. Seven rooms are available in the main house, five with private baths.

Breakfast, which may be requested in bed, consists of special warm pastry, imported cheese, seasonal fruit and tea or coffee. This is truly a chance to spend some time in another century.

Some guests enjoy breakfast on the brick patio in pleasant weather. Located on the side of the inn, the patio is surrounded by a white fence and boxwoods. A cottage with a private bath is located near the patio and available for rent. On Talbot Street, the Kemp House Inn is within footsteps of St. Michaels' shops, pubs and museums.

The building opened under the name Smithton Inn in April 1982 after Allen Smith restored it. Current on site manager, Pat Evans, has been working since September of that year.

She mentioned that the white brick edifice had been vacant for a brief time and also had served as a funeral parlor before becoming an inn.

While stressing that she is a non-believer in ghosts, Pat said that she would share a few stories from other workers and guests about the building's friendly spiritual resident.

One young worker was in the hall at the bottom of the stairway, when she said she saw a blue streak flash by and head up the stairs.

"Then, she said, 'It must be Joseph, heading up the stairs,'" Pat recounted, explaining that the ghost

is often referred to as Joseph, because that was the name of the original owner, Joseph Kemp.

"The girl was never afraid of him", Pat recalled, "In fact, she said he was just a friendly little guy."

Pat pointed out that nearly all of the unusual activity seems to occur in the Blue Room.

"In the daytime, it's quite relaxing. But in the evenings, it makes me a little uneasy. There's a different feeling," she remarked.

Pat is not the only one who senses something odd. When her daughter-in-law, Diana, was helping at the inn, the younger woman said she heard a door slam when there was no one else in the building. The worker who had seen the blue streak also complained that towels on shelves in the laundry area were tossed down on top of the washer. "Oh, Joseph's been messing around", she would say.

During the Christmas holidays, two women guests brought gifts to share. After they made the exchange, they went out to dinner. When they came back, the wrappings, which they had placed in the trash can were all over the floor.

"Maybe," said Pat, "we have a playful, little Christmas ghost here, too."

All these incidents occurred in the same room and were experienced by people who never had any contact with each other. Moreover, they all happened a year or two apart.

The last event involved a father and son in the Blue Room. The older man was in the four poster bed and the man in his 20's was sleeping in the trundle bed that pulled out from beneath the mattress.

"The father said he awoke in the middle of the night," Pat said."He thought someone was getting in bed with him. He could feel the pressure causing the queen mattress to sink, and he thought his son had gone to the bathroom and had forgotten to get back into the lower bed. But, then, the gentleman looked over and saw his son sleeping in the trundle bed and it still felt as though someone were in bed with him."

When asked how she reacts to these stories, Pat says that she just listens pleasantly, but she never tells anyone about "Joseph".

Call 410-745-2243 or write The Kemp House Inn, P.O. Box 638, St. Michaels, Md. 21663.

Photograph by Marion E. Warren

Black Walnut Point Inn

Black Walnut Point Inn Bed and Breakfast on the Chesapeake Bay offers guests the ultimate setting to truly "get away from it all." Located on the southernmost tip of Tilghman Island, the Inn is majestically situated on a 57 acre wildlife preserve that is more like a sanctuary for humans. Guests can enjoy the tranquillity of sunrise over the Choptank River and spectacular sunsets over the Chesapeake Bay.

From early land records, Black Walnut Point comprised more than 250 acres and was a fruit farm with extensive orchards. It was purchased in 1843 from Tench Tilghman (grandson of the aide-de-camp to George Washington) by Mr. John Valliant, a Baltimore merchant, who built the original house. It was one of the earliest residences built on the Island and is presently the oldest building on Tilghman. Its design was similar to three other farm houses in the Choptank River area.

By early 1900, Black Walnut Point had eroded to such an extent, that Arthur Willis, the owner, no longer farmed the land and was forced to move the house northward on the property. Since it was no longer valuable as a farm, Black Walnut Point was purchased in the 1930's as a business retreat by the Edgecomb Steel Company. It was used as a hunting and fishing lodge until 1962 when it was leased to the Russian Embassy as a get-a-way for their Washington based personnel.

Today the house features simplicity and homey comforts with appropriate furnishings, large living room with fireplace, sunroom, formal dining room with fireplace, four bedrooms with private baths and a main porch, complete with rocking chairs. One may also choose a waterfront cottage on the Riverfront complete with screened porch.

The Inn continues the property's 20th century tradition of offering its guests relaxation surrounded by nature's beauty. Walking trails, nature hikes, and waterside hammocks for bird and waterfowl watching fill a contemplative pace free of artificial distractions. The Inn also provides plenty of activities: swimming, tennis, bicycling, sightseeing, photography, fishing and boating.

So whether you just want to relax by the pool, laze around in a hammock, read a book by the fireplace or enjoy the many beautiful attractions of Talbot County, Black Walnut Point Inn is the perfect choice.

Tom and Brenda Ward, Innkeepers, look forward to making your visit a memorable one. Please call 410-886-2452 for information and reservations or write, P.O. Box 308, Tilghman Island, Md. 21671.

Photograph by Marion E. Warren

The Inn at Christmas Farm

The gift to you of The Inn at Christmas Farm is total relaxation and fascination. Dating back to 1800, the Main House holds the enchantment of a story book or the Nut Cracker Suite. The parlor of the Main House shimmers with holiday lights and cascading chandeliers. A sun porch lies just beyond where sumptuous breakfasts are served on a farm table overlooking the entrancing water view. Breakfast specialties feature French recipes, including French Apple Cake warm from the oven, shirred eggs that are farm fresh, genuine maple syrups and fresh blueberry muffins. The inn is owned by Beatrice and David Lee.

Outside is a wonderland in which to lose ones cares. A Blue Heron lifts off the water and soars across a cornfield, followed by a Snowy Egret. A peacock perches on a chimney, sweeping its tail over the roof line of the farmhouse. A graceful swan whirls out of the tall marsh grasses to glide upon the serene expanse of water.

These are a few of the sights that await you as you breakfast in the morning at Christmas Farm. A morning walk lets you explore the menagerie of sheep, peacocks, chickens and two horses, "Look" and a miniature Arabian named "James". Then, stroll out across the fields of golden corn and bright gladiolus that stretch along Cummings Creek on the Bay Hundred Peninsula about seven miles south of St. Michaels. The peninsula was so named by early English colonists following the medieval custom of forming districts wherever ten estates could support a hundred soldiers.

Christmas farm's fields have been continuously tilled since a log cabin was first built on the land about 1700. The Palmer family harvested the fields and oyster beds for 50 years before they opened the Inn in 1985, and they have let all of the improvements blend in naturally. Even the new spring-fed swimming pond follows the curve of the creek. Afternoons "poolside" are a favorite with guests.

Christmas Farm offers four elegantly furnished, air conditioned suites, each with a sitting area, private bath and king-size bed. Two are located in the Main House, and the other two in St. James Chapel, a charming 1893 building which was rescued and moved to the farm from the nearby village of Sherwood.

Several different accommodations await you:

Brother Palmer's Still was added to the Main House after the Civil War and has a wood stove and French doors that open onto the sun porch. Hidden in the floor above was the still which helped keep the farm afloat during Prohibition.

Christmas Cottage, known also as the Honeymoon Cottage, is a two-storey suite, attached to the Main House with a jacuzzi and separate entrance of antique double Dutch doors. It was built as a waterman's cottage about 1890 and moved from nearby Stone Eagle.

The Gabriel Suite in the Chapel opens through French doors onto a deck with views of fields, woods, marshes and creek. A hand carved angel with trumpet presides over the suite, which contains pieces from the owners' collection of farm furniture.

The Bell Tower Suite in the Chapel is entered from a vestibule after you pass through magnificent double church doors to a suite with canopy bed, a bar

sink and refrigerator and a brick patio with a water view of creek and pond. Its separate entry hall is popular with guests as a place to keep bicycles for touring the Bay Hundred Peninsula.

Dotted with 18th century farmsteads and watermen's hamlets, the Bay Hundred extends south to Tilghman Island, home to many of the region's remaining oyster fleet of skipjacks, the largest in the nation.

Bustling St. Michaels, known as "the town that fooled the British" during the war of 1812, offers antique stores, historic houses and the Chesapeake Bay Maritime Museum's extensive collection of boats and other nautical artifacts. Whether you want to sight-see, shop, dine on international fare and Eastern Shore delights or just swing in a hammock, Christmas Farm is close to all of these enjoyments. This fanciful inn will envelop you in its magical blend of softness in the air and stillness of the countryside. In a serenity accented only by the calling of songbirds and the faint sounding of a buoy in the Bay, your most fantastic dreams will come true at the entrancing Inn at Christmas Farm. For reservations, please call 410-745-3891.

The Swan Point Inn

The Swan Point Inn, located on rolling green lawns at Rock Hall Avenue (Rt. 20) and Coleman Road in the sleepy town of Rock Hall, known for that tasty little crustacean, the hard shell crab, is under new ownership this year. The new owners, Diane Carey and Chef Sandra Ealy, have created a lovely Inn and restaurant with the addition of sidewalks, and parking lot.

Professional lighting and landscaping now highlight a spacious new deck, which overlooks Swan Creek. The deck is kissed by the sun in the morning and shaded by huge old trees in the evening. This makes al fresco dining or sipping refreshing beverages at the deck bar very pleasurable experiences.

The inn was formerly a waterman's home-tavern/cum restaurant, frequented by local watermen of the area. It boasts a colorful history of the time when watermen went out fishing, crabbing or oystering and came back with a catch big enough to pay off a mortgage. These were the people who spent their leisure time drinking and bragging or sometimes going into the kitchen to prepare their own special recipes for all to sample.

The inn was sold several years ago and has been transformed into a charming upscale restaurant with an intimate cocktail lounge and impeccably clean, sumptuous, rooms on the upper floors. Each room has a private bath, color television, ceiling fans and air conditioning.

The rooms are tastefully decorated with large comfortable beds, plenty of closet space and wall to wall carpeting. Two rooms overlook Swan Creek. One is an efficiency for guests wishing for cooking privileges. The other two rooms overlook the sunset through the trees.

The inn has a new menu, featuring Eastern Shore specialties with an emphasis on innovative recipes, reflecting the European training of Chef Ealy, who studied at the Ecole Hotelur in Lausanne, Switzerland and attended Johnson & Wales University in Providence R.I. for pastry training. She also attended Rutgers University and received her B.S. Degree in education from Glassboro State College of New Jersey. She has taught culinary arts in a vocational high school for thirteen years before retiring and purchasing the Swan Point Inn.

Photograph by Marion E. Warren

Some of the chef's personal favorites include Escargot in Puff Pastry with burgundy sauce, fresh Flounder Imperial, prepared en croute, and Flounder Florentine with fresh spinach and cheese in twin roulades, broiled and glazed with mornay sauce. Chicken Chesapeake, a delightful entree of boneless breast of chicken, stuffed with crab, is broiled to perfection and topped with asparagus spears, Swiss cheese and sauce Smitane, a light cream sauce characterized by a hint of tarragon and sour cream.

The new owners recognize that many of today's diners are looking for lighter fare and have developed entrees that meet those requests. The new menu offers several "on the light side" items, including Petite Filets, Petite Crab dinners and the wonderful signature salad, which is perfect for a warm summer evening: Julienne of chicken is served over a bed of crisp, mixed greens, grated sharp cheese, sliced Granny Smith apples, wedges of hard cooked eggs, and garnish of tomato, croutons and Bermuda onion rings.

The menu also offers an exciting range of veal dishes and the weekend specialty, Prime Rib, blackened in king size, and cut to order. Daily fish specials, when available, include Fresh Tuna, Cajun Catfish, Mahi Mahi with mango sauce, and Imperial Soft Shell Crabs.

The two lovely dining rooms are candle lit and decorated tastefully with art from local artists and potters. The decor is soothing and pleasing to the eye, and the pictured back room is private and available for special functions and banquets. The inn is an ideal place for a business luncheon,sales seminar or workshop, and the staff is very accommodating and helpful in planning any function.

Whether you dine al fresco on the deck or in one of the dining rooms. The Swan Point Inn makes your every dream come true for superb dining and gracious lodging. For reservations and all catering needs call 410-639-2500.

Moonlight Bay

A visit to Moonlight Bay Marina and Inn is an opportunity to envision the past, while enjoying the comforts and amenities of an elegantly appointed luxury inn. A drive to the end of Rock Hall Avenue (Route 20) with a right turn to tree lined Lawton Avenue, will take you to the only bed and breakfast in Rock hall nestled on the shores of the Chesapeake Bay.

Located in one of the last working watermen's towns, Moonlight Bay, with its panorama of pristine waters provides one with the fullness of nature's beauty in a country setting.

The original house, constructed in the mid 1800's, was once used as a ferry stop for passengers and freight. Livestock and produce were transported to Baltimore from this point as well as vacationers, seeking the serenity of the Eastern Shore. For many years, it was the home of the Gratitude, Maryland Post Office.

In later years, the building was used as a restaurant called the "Shady Rest".

After the owner passed away, the restaurant was sold, sub divided into apartments and later abandoned.

Its metamorphosis began in January of 1992, when Dorothy and Bob Santangelo purchased the property and transformed the building and grounds into the beautiful Moonlight Bay Marina and Inn of today.

From the 50 slip marina, up the rolling lawns to the enchanting English Gardens, one is captivated by the exterior surroundings. With central air conditioning and private baths, the inn offers five uniquely decorated guest rooms, each with its own ambience, retaining the charm of their historic surroundings.

When the sun greets you each morning with a spectacular view of the Bay, your hosts, Dorothy and Bob also greet you with a full breakfast. The day offers guests many various opportunities to enjoy leisure activities, while late afternoon is highlighted by the serving of English High Tea.

As dusk visits this vacation paradise, the sun dips on the horizon, and another magnificent day at Moonlight Bay has come to an end.

To speak with the inn keeper, phone 410-639-2660 or write to Moonlight Bay Marina and Inn, 6002 Lawton Avenue, Rockhall, Md. 21661.

Photograph by Marion E. Warren

Huntingfield

Huntingfield is located on a peninsula called "Eastern Neck". These Peninsulas are formed by the many sluggish rivers and estuaries that flow into the Chesapeake Bay. The name for this particular peninsula is curious since Eastern Neck is the most western of all of the necks created by the tributaries of the Chester River. Eastern Neck has also been documented as being called "Huntingfield" since the 1650's. The Eastern Neck (Huntingfield) shores were the bountiful home of Nanicoke Indians who hunted, fished, and planted the fruitful soil. In the 1650's, it is recorded that this peninsula, was included in a land grant given by Lord Baltimore to Thomas Ringgold who named it "Huntingfield". The land and fields were (and are) flat and were easy to clear and are ideal for growing tobacco, small grains, corn, beans, and vegetables. To this day, Huntingfield (Eastern Neck) is one of richest producing agriculture areas in the country. Over the years, from the 1650's to the present, Thomas Ringgold's land has been divided and subdivided, and sold and resold until only a small portion is still called "Huntingfield". One such section, comprised of 70 acres of farm, forest and wet-land, is located at the east end of Huntingfield Creek and is, at present, called Huntingfield Manor. History describes a Chesapeake Bay that was narrower and deeper than the present Chesapeake Bay. It has been reported that as much as 900 feet of Huntingfield Point, has eroded into Huntingfield Creek and the Bay. Huntingfield Creek was, at one time, deep enough to handle sailing ships and packet boats from Annapolis and Baltimore. When such ships could not, because of wind and current, make Swan Creek and the Haven, they would anchor in Huntingfield Creek and use the horses and buggies kept at Huntingfield Manor when it was known as "the Prevention of Inconvenience".

The main house of Huntingfield Manor is, at present, a bed and breakfast. You approach the main house by way of a 650 ft lane, lined with twenty-two flowering Bradford Pear Trees. At the end of the lane rests the "telescoped" house with tall columns framing the front door. The center or the peak of the house is the oldest part and undated. In the 1940's, the house was given a face life while a garage and "Mother-in-law" rooms were added. Also at or about this time, a small cottage was built behind and separate from the main house.

In the mid eighties, the house was again refurbished with the addition of six bathrooms and a laundry room. Today, the main house is one hundred thirty six feet long and one room (24 feet) wide. George and Bernadine Starken, the present owners, are again renovating Huntingfield Manor. The south end of the main house is currently a screened, three-season porch. The Red Room contains the large fireplace and presents a cozy spot to read or a place to discuss one's philosophy. Just off the Reading room,

the next room in line going from south to north, you enter a kitchen with two walls of windows, which presents the view of the magnificent fields and wooded tracts that protect the mouth of the Huntingfield Creek. Further north of the Reading Room lies the Breakfast Room. Beyond this room, lie two ground floor bedrooms. Four other bedrooms above the ground floor complete the makeup of the main house. The Starken's enjoy sharing the beauty, the wildlife and the peace and tranquility of Huntingfield Manor with their B & B guests. Call 4l0-639-7779 for reservations.

Photograph by Marion E. Warren

Lauretum Inn Bed & Breakfast

The Lauretum Inn Bed & Breakfast is located on the edge of Chestertown on Md. Rt. 20 on the way to historic Rock Hall, a waterman's community. Turn to the right up its curving road to see a magnificent edifice on six shaded acres. Just two minutes from downtown Chestertown, the Inn is within easy access of all of the many area attractions. If you come by boat, the Lauretum Inn's van will pick you up at the dock. The original owner, U.S. Senator George Vickers (1801-1879), lovingly built this gracious country manor and named it Lauretum Place or "Laurel Grove", the name of a place on the Aventine Hill in Ancient Rome.

Born in Chestertown, Senator Vickers was one of 21 Whig members of the Senatorial College. During the Civil war, he was appointed Major General of the Maryland Militia by the Governor. In 1868, he became a U.S. Senator and subsequently voted for the acquittal of President Andrew Johnson on impeach-

Photograph by Marion E. Warren

ment charges. Legend has it that the Johnson impeachment vote was deadlocked and a messenger was sent to Senator Vicker's home because he was ill. His written vote was hand delivered and decisive in overturning the impeachment.

The Lauretum Inn Bed & Breakfast features a lovely screened in porch, a charming central hallway in Williamsburg blue with white trim, original plaster ceiling medallions, fireplaces with elegantly restored mantels and newly decorated rooms in the period of Vickers' time. An eloquent staircase, tucked behind the reading room, rises three stories. Three rooms are on the second floor and two suites on the third floor with private and semi-private baths. Stained glass in the windows casts a picturesque shadow in the sunlight.

Your hosts and co-owners, Peg and Bill Sites, are parents to 20 children and have 59 grand and great-grand children and are well accustomed to caring for many guests. The inn is perfect for a small informal business meeting. A gourmet continental breakfast with prize winning jams is a sumptuous treat.

Whether your visit includes business, touring, hunting fishing, boating, bicycling or just getting completely away from it all, a stay at the Lauretum Inn affords the luxury of country Victorian surroundings and warm hospitality. Call Peg or Bill at 1-800-742-3236 for information and availability.

Kent County

Kent County is far from the hustle bustle of maddening crowds on a peninsula on Maryland's Eastern Shore. The sweeping panorama of the Chesapeake Bay is on the West, the Sassafras River on the North and the beautiful Chester River on the South. Located on Rt. 213 just off Rt. 50 over the Bay Bridge, it is a lovely trip down winding roads to Chestertown. Established in 1706 as the County Seat, the old town was visited by Washington 8 times from 1756 - 1793. On its three walking tours per year, in May, September and December, tours of historic homes and inns are given. The Chestertown "Tea Party" commemorates the town's rebellion against the King's tax on tea.

See photos of more colonial homes of the Eastern Shore on page 32

White Swan Tavern

The White Swan Tavern at 231 High Street in Historic Chestertown was built in 1730. This precisely restored 18th century inn, the epitome of a colonial tavern of Maryland, is a brick two storey building with pillared front porch. The original door, with authentic graining, opens to a center hallway with old flooring, leading to a foyer and the inn keeper's desk. This foyer gives out onto a lovely garden and patio for breakfasts and tea.

To the right as one enters is a dining room with tables for games or high teas. The front stairs are near this doorway, and a map of the Chesapeake in colonial times graces the wall. These interesting maps may be seen throughout the inn. The dining room has a Celia series of colonial cartoon prints on its plastered walls. Windsor chairs complement the tables. A powder horn and Flintlock pistol hang over the mantel.

To the left of the entrance is a parlor with tables and a secretary desk, which is a reproduction by Evans of one at Colonial Williamsburg.

The grandfather's clock on the front wall, made in 1740 in Boston by Joseph Medley, has the information about its creation inside its door, which is ornately carved and painted in an Oriental motif.

This room is often used for private parties. The window seats under swag valances lend themselves to such functions, when tables and chairs are removed for dancing or buffets. Corner cupboards conserve space.

Walking down the central hallway, we find a lovely sitting room on the left. In vivid hues of aqua and yellow, it is a cheerful room for reading, chatting or watching television. The furnishings are covered in yellow and aqua, and the bright aqua molding and mantel are original to the building.

Guests sip white wine in this parlor before dining out. Working fireplaces in these first floor rooms provide a cozy atmosphere in inclement seasons.

Continental breakfast, complementary wine, and a fruit basket are included in the room rates. Breakfast is served on the patio when weather permits.

Highlights of an archeological dig on the property displayed in well lighted glass cases include sketches, artifacts and instructive labels, describing colonial objects discovered.

Four elegant rooms are upstairs and two suites, all have private baths. The inn keeper is up to receive you until 10 p.m. A telephone is in the foyer and a parking lot is behind this impeccable AAA approved 3 diamond inn. Call the gracious manager, Mary, at 410-778-2300.

Geddes Piper House

The Geddes Piper House on Church Alley is the home of the Historical Society. In 1774, the lot was sold to William Geddes, the customs collector for Chestertown's port. The house was reputed to have been built by Geddes soon after. In 1784, Geddes sold the house to James Piper, a merchant, and it was in his family until 1834, when it was sold to the Westcott family. It remained in that family until 1914.

In the living room is a beautifully restored desk from 1770, an heirloom of the Wescotts. A portrait of Rebecca Brown Ringgold, wife of Thomas Jefferson Ringgold hangs in the back parlor. Samuel Ringgold's portrait hangs in the front parlor. A lithograph of his death in the Mexican War is nearby.

Another portrait is of Senator George Vickers, who cast the deciding vote against Andrew Johnson's impeachment. His home was at the site of the Lauretum Inn. Swords in the dining room belong to George Vickers and his son.

The front section of the house was the original portion and the back section was added in the 1830s.

A display in the basement kitchen includes an apple butter tub large cabbage shredder, butter churn and beaten biscuit recipe.

Biscuits had no leavening except air and were beaten 20 minutes for the family and 30 minutes for company.

Upstairs in one room, depicting the 1800's, is a child's riding habit, a Windsor chair from the 1700's, a Wescott family piece and a copper bracelet from Paris. A red, white and blue coverlet, made in 1842 bears the name of its maker.

The front bedroom displays a patchwork quilt on the four poster bed, and a crazy quilt. The wedding dress of Sophia Ringgold illustrates how petite women were. She married Nathaniel Hynson, and lived nearby. In the hallway is a 1907 view of Chestertown. An 1860 map of Kent County hangs in the lower hall.

The Geddes Piper House is open to the public on weekends from May to October and by appointment. The Candlelight tour of Chestertown in September always features the House. For information, call 410-778-3499.

Modernized Maryland Beaten Biscuits
with baking powder added...

1 1/2 lb. flour	1 c. water
1/2 tsp. salt	1/2 c. shortening
1 tsp. baking powder	

Mix all ingredients together. Beat with mallet until smooth and it snaps. Bake at 500 about ten minutes. If browning too fast, reduce heat and finish baking. In all baking time is about 18 - 20 minutes.

Wide Hall

In Chestertown at 101 Water Street on the bank of the Chester River, is Widehall, one of the most beautiful homes in Maryland. Of brick and two stories with a high basement, it has dormer windows and a two storey porch, commanding a fine view across the river.

Thomas Smyth bought the lot from the heirs of an estate, one of whom was only 20 and could not legally convey the title. Smyth secured the title from the Colonial Assembly.

The front door is approached by two flights of steps with a brick terrace and opens on the wide hall running the depth of the building to the garden door, on the river porch with its beautiful columns.

On the left of the front door is the stair hall from which a hanging staircase leads to upper floors. Separating the halls are three arches. Another arch divides the main hall in half. On the right of the front door is the large drawing room, lighted by tall windows. The fireplace here has been restored, and the one in the dining room has panelling to the ceiling. near Wall-of Troy molding which is quite lovely.

Widehall is listed on the National Register as well as being within the National Historic Landmark District.

Claddaugh Farm

Claddaugh Farm is a Victorian farm house, ninety two years old, located near the entrance to historic Chestertown. It takes its name from a town in Ireland and its romantic aura from a legend of the famous author James Joyce's ancestor, who was sold into slavery. During that time he trained to be a goldsmith of great artistry and imagination. He created a crest with hands symbolizing friendship. The two hands hold a heart (love) beneath a crown (loyalty).

The goldsmith, Richard Joyce, a 16th century fisherman, was captured by Algerian pirates, the very

week he was to be married. During his captivity, he fashioned a ring with these symbols for the fiance who awaited him. After years of waiting, Richard was released and journeyed home to find that the love he thought would surely be gone was still longing for his return.

The pillars at the entrance to the inn bear this romantic emblem. A short lane will take you to the lovely old house where you will be received warmly. A spacious dining room is on one side of the foyer with a long table for breakfasts. On the left side is a drawing room for playing games, reading or watching television. Fireplaces in both rooms make for a cozy atmosphere.

Spacious guest rooms are named after counties in Ireland, and guests awaken to a complete Continental breakfast of cereal, fruit, homemade muffins, juice coffee or tea. The country inn offers 4 guest rooms and one suite. They are bright and beautifully decorated. Many high windows keep them full of light. The top floor dormer rooms share a bath, and all the others are equipped with private baths. The friendly family ownership also offers miniature horses and kennels for your hunting dogs.

This is a conveniently located and enchanting inn with cordial hosts. Call Florence at 410-778-4894 or (800)-328-4894 for more information.

"So inscrutable is the arrangement of causes and consequences in this world, that a two-penny duty on tea, unjustly imposed in a sequestered part of it, changes the condition of all its inhabitants." Thomas Jefferson

---

Imperial Hotel

The Imperial Hotel is the epitome of a true turn-of-the-century hostelery. Built in 1903 by Wilbur W. Hubbard, a prominent Chestertown resident, it is located in the historic district at 208 High Street, back to back with the Geddes Piper House, home of the Kent County Historical Society.

The garden between the two is perfect for weddings or conferences. A conference room offers a changing art show and has a large conference table. Jazz nights are held in this garden setting on Friday evenings. The Geddes Piper House is sometimes used as a meeting space for conferences held at the hotel.

The hotel building was placed on the National Register of Historic Places in 1984, and the house underwent a painstaking restoration just after that time. The work won an award from the Maryland Trust for Historic Preservation and multiple awards for the interior design by H. Chambers Company.

Easy to distinguish as one drives up the main street of town, the hotel's wide welcoming verandas are typical of the Chestertown old homes. The sign says "Hotel Imperial", because the historic photos show that the hotel had a similar sign early in its history, and only a historical sign could be approved.

Guests can walk out on verandas from guest rooms, decorated in a luxurious Victorian style, featuring strong, bold colors and patterns in floral prints and stripes. Each bedroom has its own distinctive charm and motif. Amenities include color cable television, complimentary toiletries, and towel warmers.

In an upstairs parlor guests can have private parties or just chat or play checkers. A continental breakfast is served to guests in the Fountain Dining Room.

The two dining rooms on either side of the front door are very different in motif. The Fountain Room to the left of the foyer is in mauve and soft lavender shades with beautiful Victorian chairs and tables, while the one to the right of the foyer is in dark hunter green and plaid with hunting prints gracing the walls. Although one might think the rooms suggest formality, guests are encouraged to dress rather informally. Hunters often come in from the field and boaters in the boating togs come from the water.

The inn has repeatedly been judged third best inn in the five state Mid Atlantic area by the Zagat Survey and the prestigious Wine Spectator Magazine has given it the Award of Excellence. Wine tastings are often held at the inn with visiting chefs complementing the skills of Executive Chef Rodney Scruggs, who has won national acclaim for his creative ingenuity.

The presentation of each dish is exquisite and portions are generous. Begin your repast with such appetizers as Poached Oysters and Country Ham, spinach and tomatoes in puff pastry with dill butter sauce or Baked Brie wrapped in Phyllo with Granny Smith apples and walnuts on a bed of wild greens.

Enjoy salads from the salad chef, nurtured in her own garden and served in such combinations as Mixed Baby Greens with Mango, sugared Almonds tossed in a vanilla vinaigrette. Warm up with Sweet Local White Corn Bisque with beans and fresh cilantro or a similar delicious soup such as Southwestern Gazpacho, topped with jumbo lump crabmeat.

Entrees might include such delicacies as Sauteed Alaskan Coho Salmon with Artichokes, Black Cured Olives and tomato concasse, fresh basil and tomato coulis. Grilled Filet Mignon might be offered with Grilled Oyster Mushrooms, leeks, stoneground mustard, and a thyme sherry vinegar sauce. Sauteed Alaskan Halibut might appear with Maine Lobster Meat and a white corn red potato hash in dill butter sauce.

In spite of all this plentitude, be certain to leave room for the "piece de resistance", Lisa Leclerc Scruggs delectable pastries. They are incomparable. She studied under the White House pastry chef, Roland Mesiner. Her Imperial Chocolate Praline Triangle with Grand Marnier sauce is a signature dish, which is celestial! Or for a lighter finale, enjoy an Orange Zested Cheesecake, wrapped in a crepe with raspberry coulis, for example.

The menu changes every two or three months. A reasonably priced wine list accompanies the regular one and vintages are recommended for each menu item by the congenial"maitre d'hotel", Robb Kimbles or by gracious owners, Barbara and Bob Lavelle, who have owned the inn for two years.

Call Robb at (410) 778-5000 for special catering or conference requests or to plan the wedding of your dreams at the superbly romantic Imperial Hotel.

Rock Hall

"Those who expect to reap the blessings of freedom must, like men, undergo the fatiques of supporting it."
Thomas Paine.

The quaint fishing village, 20 miles from Chestertown on Rt. 20, was originally known as Rock Hall Crossroads, established in 1707, Many believe that this collection of homes dates further back in history. Trumpington, Huntingfield and Wickcliffe were awarded by the crown to their prospective owners by 1659. East Neck Island and New Yarmouth were the locations of the earliest settlements in Kent County. New Yarmouth at Gray's Inn Creek was the political center. In 1697, the court was moved to what is now Chestertown.

Washington, Madison and Jefferson travelled through Rock Hall often. It was an important port for packets bringing people from the South and Western Shore to inland routes headed north to Philadelphia and New York. Water routes were often the safest.

For over 300 years, locals have earned their living from the water which is pleasurable for fishermen and boaters. The Town Museum in the Municipal building and the Waterman's Museum next to Haven Harbour Marina offer a closer view of Rock Hall's history. Nature lovers enjoy the abundance of wildlife on East Neck Island, a federal wildlife refuge since the 1960's. Remington Farms, another refuge, draws naturalists. Remington Day in September is an all day event featuring wildlife. Rock Hall's "Ferry Park" affords some of the most splendid sunsets in the area.

Trumpington

Five miles from Rock Hall is Trumpington, which has been in the Thomas Smythe family for more than three centuries. The Smythes were very prominent in Colonial and Revolutionary times and were members of the Provincial Council, judges of the Provincial Court, Burgesses of Kent and justices for the county, all before 1694. They also married into the Tilghman family when Sarah, daughter of Thomas Smythe, married Matthew Tilghman.

Trumpington is one of the oldest land grants in present day Kent County. It was deeded in 1658.

The present owners are Mr. and Mrs. Robert H. Strong, Sr., and Mrs. Strong is the three greats granddaughter of Thomas Smythe, who acquired Trumpington for 6,000 lbs.of tobacco in 1687.

The house was here when Anna Maria Smythe married Dr. Thomas Willson, Mrs. Strong's great, great grandfather. and at present, 365 of the original 400 acres are still intact. The Strongs are still farming the land. In 1979 Trumpington was protected when it was accepted to The National Register of Historical Places.

Named for a town in Cambridge, England, the plantation house retains much of the history of the area in its fourteen rooms and grounds. Matthew Tilghman, Sarah and their children are all buried in the cemetery. Matthew, son of Edward by his wife Julianna Carroll, was the speaker of the house of Delegates in 1791. The family owned several farms between Chestertown and Rock Hall.

The first house was destroyed by fire and replaced by another in 1723 by Thomas Smythe. The existence of an early structure was confirmed when the orogonal foundation was found beneath the basement of the present house.

Nine of the 14 rooms have wide old-fashioned fireplaces and all partition walls are of solid brick. The wainscotting and carved crown moldings are in a fine state of preservation. The banisters and railing of the broad stairway leading to the third floor are of solid mahogany.

The entrance hall is graced with framed copies of land grants signed by Horatio Sharp, Governor of the Province (1753-1769). (Originals were donated to the archives in Annapolis) Iron hooks near the front door cradle an old musket, and a sabre. A "Case Clock" made in Wales stands in the hall with pictures of the family "coats-of-Arms". A portrait of Colonel Thomas Smythe III, son of Thomas Smythe II and his wife, Mary Ann Ringgold, also hangs here. Bound to James Calder, a prominent lawyer to learn the law, he became a judge and one of the delegates sent to the Provincial Convention with William Ringgold, Joseph Earle, and Thomas Hands, father-in-law of Col. Thomas Smythe. They formed the association of Free Men of Maryland, whose Declaration hangs in the State House at Annapolis. Thomas Smythe was also a trustee of Washington College, founded in 1782 in Chestertown.

A beautiful porch looks out on a vista of the Bay and was used as the front of the house.

In the parlor the flooring does not show nails as in the hall and pictures of ancestors link the generations. Bubbled window panes have signatures and dates scrawled by diamonds.

In the parlor was a chapel where priests performed ceremonies. A linen press, belonging to Thomas Smyth was used to store vestments. The altar rail and original altar are now near the chapel.

The tapestry on the wall is a Scotch ingrain, c. 1875-1890. Mrs. Strong hooked the carpet, covering the steps, with the family names on them. Several paintings of Trumpington and a pettipoint by the Strong's youngest daughter, Rose Marie, adorn the walls. The floor of the dining room was brick until 1924.

The kitchen is believed to be the oldest part of the house. It was a separate building. Brick flooring was removed from the kitchen in 1924. In 1979, the fireplace was re-opened and an old iron crane was found inside. The kitchen joists were charred black with cooking and the walls were very rough and covered with horsehair plaster.

The second floor reveals four bedrooms with a "Baltimore" bed in one. Throughout the bedrooms are heirlooms to let you see how this family remained steadfast during troubled times.

Trumpington Ladies Crunchy Chocolate Biscuits

4 oz. butter 6 T.	3 T. sugar
6 T.Dark Corn Syrup	1/2 lb. honey grahams
2 T. Cocoa	

Melt butter, sugar, and syrup over low heat. Do not boil. Add cocoa and mix well. Remove from heat; stir in crushed and broken honey grahams. Press into well greased square pan. Cool overnight, cut and serve.

Hinchingham

One of Kent County's grandest homes is Hinchingham, on the shore of the Bay, a two and a half storey mansion. Built in 1774, Hinchingham is one of the largest colonal residences in the county.

In 1659, Thomas Hynson was granted 2200 acres of land. By the mid-19th century it had been divided into nine smaller parcels. The largest, containing 700 acres, belonged to William Frisby who inherited the land from his father in 1738. William Frisby deeded 200 acres to his brother, James. During the sixty years that James owned the property the house was built. The date of construction, 1774, appears in large numerals on the southern end of the house.

The Frisbys were descendants of the famous Augustine Herrmann of Bohemia Manor in Cecil County who created the map of the entire area and directed the building of the canal there.

Hinchingham is a 309 acre working farm, circa 1774, located near Tolchester Beach Road. It offers a 1,900 feet frontage on the Bay. The brick floor in the kitchen still remains as does the curving servants' staircase. 12 rooms include a beautiful entrance hall and a room with pine flooring, fireplace and china closets, probably the dining room. The library and present dining room have fireplaces. Four bedrooms are on the second floor and two on the top floor.

The property was restored by Carolene Hynson du Pont, descendant of the patentee, in the 1930's and in 1987 and 1988 the house was restored, renovated and modernized under the direction of architect Wayne Good, AIA.

Georgetown

Georgetown, a popular port area north of Chestertown, has many interesting homes of the 18th century. Beside the historic Kitty Knight House is "the yellow house" with Duck Hollow across from it, a tall two story brick home with beautiful gardens. It is named for the inlet where ducks swim below it. Across the river over the bridge, is a large house.

Near Union Folly Road, it was at one time in line with the old bridge. These are all private homes.

Georgetown was a base of Continental supplies from 1775-1783, a port of entry and ferry landing. It was burned by the British on May 6, 1813.

The Carrousel Horse Inn at 145 Main street in Galena, located in the north of Kent County a mile from the Sassafras River on Highway 213. The white frame house with lovely grounds and gardens beyond is on 3 grassy acres and accommodates guests in a warm ambiance of period furniture suited to the c. 1880 renovation. Seasonal amenities include fireplaces in intimate sitting rooms and large shaded porch for breakfast and reading. Call 410-648-5476.

The Rose Hill B & B is on a miniature rose farm just up the road from Galena near Cecil County at 13842 Gregg Neck Road near the Heritage farms. A wide deck offers a lovely view as does the Garden Room. On the first floor is a guest room with brass bed. Full breakfasts are served in the pleasant dining room or on the deck. Call 410-648-5334.

Kitty Knight House

"When I contemplate the natural dignity of Man; when I feel for the honor and happiness of its character, I become irritated at the attempt to govern mankind by force and fraud, as if they were all knaves and fools, and can scarcely avoid disgust at those who are thus imposed upon." Thomas Paine

Kitty Knight House rises in stately fashion just above the Georgetown Yacht Basin on the Sassafras river. The inn dates back to the 1700's. The original owner, a female maverick, saved the house from the British during the invasion of 1813.

Born into a prominent family in 1755, Catherine Knight, left the family home at the age of 16 to lead a life of her own. Her father, knowing the headstrong nature of his only daughter, purchased a house for her, which is now the Kitty Knight House. Often described as "one of the most beautiful women ever born and raised in Kent county," Kitty Knight's regal stature dazzled many, including George Washington, with whom she claimed to have danced. Yet, she is renowned for her heroism rather than for being a society belle.

In May 1813, when the British troops advanced up the Sassafras river, burning and looting towns, Georgetown residents fled, but Kitty Knight stood her ground to protect an invalid neighbor. Defying Admiral George Cockburn, she declared, "I shall not leave. If you burn this house, you burn me with it." After several attempts to persuade her to leave, the British finally relented.

The amazing thing about this was that she was 58 at the time and lived to be 79, remaining a strong, remarkable woman decades ahead of her time. She insisted that her tombstone should read Miss Kitty Knight, as she wanted it to be clear that she was not someone's wife.

A mural in the dining room depicts the scene of Kitty, rebelling against the British, with houses burning in the distance. Another larger painting shows Kitty as a gracious ghost, presiding over the banquet room.

She saved the house and adjacent one, which were combined into an inn with 11 guest rooms upstairs.

Two large dining rooms and a deck provide guests with elegant ambience. Chef Michael Metzger and Sous Chef Joe Burgess are talented. Enjoy such delights as Lobster stuffed Ravioli with creamy Romano Cheese sauce or Kitty Knight Crab Bisque for starters. Then, go on to Prime Rib, roasted with herbs and spices, served on weekends, or Chicken au Poivre with a five peppercorn cream sauce. Scallops Beurre Blanc, Poached Salmon with dill capper lemon butter or Blackened Tuna and Shrimp in a tangy Creole sauce are just a few of the tantalizing seafood items. Tempting desserts might include Pumpkin Cognac Cheesecake, as you succumb to the enchantment of this historic inn. Call 410-648-5777.

White House Farm

White House Farm was built in 1721, according to an inscription on its wall. Located not far from Galena, it was owned by Thomas Perkins in 1729. He was the uncle of Colonel Isaac Perkins who entertained President Washington at the house, supplied milled grain for bread for Washington's troops, owned 600 acres and he even owned part of Chestertown.

The property is now 50 acres and has an alleged resident ghost.

Mary Perkins Stewart, wife of a doctor, is buried on the property, and inaccurate legends report that her spirit is the ghost of a girl who eloped, fell from her horse, struck her head on a rock and died.

The Perkins genealogical chart shows that Mary went on to wed the physician. It was a servant girl who hit her head on the rock. Blood stains do appear on the rock could not be removed.

The house is basically the same as it was in 1721 with brick floor in the kitchen, and elegant, castle-like furniture, accented by classical caryatids. The stairways are the same curving narrow ones which Mrs. Pinder still negotiates gracefully.

When Mr. and Mrs. Pinder bought the house they were told about its ghost by previous owners.

The house was in need of restoration and the Pinders worked hard to restore it for two years.

As they painted the kitchen one night, they heard a sound as though someone was walking upstairs. They decided to leave, and on returning the next day they could find nothing strange, but mysterious footsteps have been heard after.

One evening Mr. Pinder was in the kitchen with his two dogs when he heard footsteps in the dining room. The dogs got up and went toward the dining room, stopping at the doorway growling with hackles standing up. Then, he heard the sound of retreating footsteps and a door opening and closing and went to the dining room but no one was there.

Mrs. Pinder woke one night to see a blue-night gowned figure pass through her bedroom. She thought it had been her daughter, but her daughter said that she didn't own a blue nightgown!

The Pinders invited parties of guests to White House Farm on the eve of January 8, the anniversary of the fatal ride. Local legend says that at midnight on the date, the girl will "walk again". The Pinders and their guests gathered near the stone and did hear noises, which Mrs. Pinder claims were the hootings of an owl. She welcomes people to tour the house and try to find one.

Easton

"The principles of right and wrong are legible to every reader; to pursue them requires not the aid of many counselors. The whole art of government consists in the art of being honest. Only aim to do your duty, and mankind will give you credit where you fail." Thomas Jefferson

The town of Easton is a place of charm, business importance and historical significance. It is the County Seat of Talbot County, named after Ireland's Grace Talbot, and is a shopping center for the Eastern Shore. Easton, known as "The Colonial Capital of the Eastern Shore" grew inward from the water, around a religious institution, (Third Haven Meeting House), and a court of justice.

Originally named Talbot Court House, and later Talbot Town, in 1788 the town was organized and renamed Easton. A "Cathedral Town", being the location of the Episcopal Diocese of Easton, Easton had the first newspaper on the Eastern Shore, first bank, first gas plant, first steamer line and first airplane to Baltimore.

The Historical Society of Talbot County

Journey through three centuries of tidewater history at the Historical Society in the heart of Easton.

The award winning enchanting grounds are the historic house museums of James and Joseph Neall and "End of Controversie", the faithfully reproduce 1670 house of religious pioneer Wenlock Christison.

This Quaker suffered torture and imprisonment in England and Massachusetts before arriving in Talbot County. Here, he was elected to the Maryland Assembly in 1678. His home was on the banks of Goldsborough Creek. This partial reconstruction was done by historian Dr. H. Candlee Forman, who deeded it to the Historical Society in 1984. It represents the English Tudor or late Medieval style.

Because of Charles Calvert's 17th century invitation to Quakers to settle in Maryland, the State has a legacy of common sense, tolerance and simplicity in architecture, reflected exquisitely in Joseph's Cottage. Typical of Easton houses of the 1795 period, it is a one and a half storey house with a reconstructed workshop attached. The entrance room shows carpentry samples and tools. The next small room was living space for James Neall's brother, Joseph, his apprentices and a black orphan girl helper, while the upper storey was their sleeping space. The house was built on Glenwood Avenue, then known as Carpenter

Street, and moved and restored by the Historical Society in 1976.

A fine example of Federal architecture is the James Neall House, built on South Washington Street between 1804 and 1810. The Historical Society restored it in 1962, opening it to the public for tours. Its Federal style is graceful and its tall 3 1/2 storey height was unique to Easton. The beautiful secretary in the front parlor is filled with encyclopedias read by James Neall and has his book plate in it.

The dining room parlor contains an elegant table set with Canton China. The twelve mahogany chairs were made by Annapolis cabinet maker, John Shaw.

An office/breakfast room was built by James in 1810 for business, joining the dining room with the kitchen, with an open hearth and equipment for cooking and health care.

The simple staircase in the entrance hall takes one to the second floor with its master bedroom and daughters' room. Third floor rooms for apprentices have rope beds. A large loom is on the attic floor. Ten rooms and eight fireplaces compose the house.

The award winning Historical Society Auditorium is in the Ebenezer Methodist Episcopal Church, c.1856. The original stained-glass windows and pressed tin ceiling create a unique atmosphere for weddings and conferences. Call 410-822-0773.

The Brick Hotel or Stewart Building

After Philemon Hemsley built the Court House in Easton in 1710, inns and taverns were built along Federal Street for miles.

The location became more attractive after the "new" court House was built in 1794, but in 1810 a fire swept the corner northeast of the Court House, including the house of John and Mary Kennedy.

Samuel Groome, a well-known and respected merchant, bought the Kennedy house and had it restored for his home. He had a fine brick structure built to serve as a hotel and tavern. For many years, it was known as "The Brick Hotel".

Chaffinch House Bed & Breakfast
132 S. Harrison St.
Easton, Md. 21601
1-800-861-5074

Oxford

"He has constrained our fellow-citizens, taken captive on the high seas, to bear arms against their country, to become the executioners of their friends and brethren, or to fall themselves by their hands."   Thomas Jefferson re: King George

Oxford, one of the oldest towns in Maryland, was already in existence for perhaps 20 years before it's founding in 1683. In that year it was named by the Maryland General Assembly as a seaport and laid out as a town. In 1694, Oxford and a new town, Anne Arundel (now Annapolis) were selected the only ports of entry for the province. Until the Revolution, Oxford enjoyed prominence as an international shipping center.

Early citizens included Robert Morris, Sr. who greatly influenced the town's growth. His son, Robert Morris, "the financier of the Revolution", Jeremiah Banning, war hero and statesman, Reverend Thomas Bacon, Anglican clergyman, and Matthew Tilghman, known as the "patriarch of Maryland" had homes near here.

The Academy House at 205 N. Morris Street was an officers' residence for the Maryland Military Academy from 1848-1855.

The Barnaby House at 212 N. Morris St. was built in the 1770's by Cpt. Richard Barnaby. On the grounds of Cutts & Case, Byberry, Oxford's oldest house, dating from 1695, is a typical early Oxford cottage and Calico is a Tudor style cottage.

Nichols House

The Nichol's House at 217 S. Morris Street, built by Samuel Fernandis Nichols, circa l880, is one of Oxford's landmark examples of Second Empire style architecture. It's tall mansard roof, punctuated by gable-roofed dormers and chimneys, is particularly dramatic.

Mrs. Adelaide Nichols' New York Millinery Store occupied the first floor of the house with the family's living quarters on the second floor.

The spacious double parlor, with pocket doors, matching ornate marble fireplaces and ten-foot ceilings, was the site for a wedding reception according to the March 6, 1886 edition of the Easton Gazette, which stated that the newly-weds, Miss Jennie Nichols and Mr. Harvey Montague, were honored at the home of her aunt, Adelaide Nichols, with the happy couple seated on the velvet sofa in the double parlor. The house remained in the Nichols family until l964.

Since purchasing the house in January l993, Steve and Pat Wheaton have given a facelift to the exterior by adding the original shutters, which were found in

The Nichols House

said that his grandfather came from Germany and acquired it. He has always kept Plimhimmon because of its historical significance. Tench Tilghman, is buried in the Oxford Cemetary.

Mr. Myers said that his Grandfather had built a white, low portion onto the house, now yellow painted brick. A beautiful Willow Oak over 400 years old is in the front yard. It is a National Champion Oak of 130 feet in height, registered by the Dept. of National Resources and taller than the Wye Oak.

The house is beautiful inside. It has a front portico, used for casual living. The central hallway features a lovely staircase carved with scrolls. The living room to the left of the front door contains a striking mauve satin sofa, over which are Myers family portraits.

The dining room to the right features a lovely large table and side board, both graceful English antiques. Mr. and Mrs. Myers love their home and are afraid it will be sold to developers eventually. This is a private home, not open to the public.

St. Michaels

St. Michaels is called the town that fooled the British. When it was being attacked in 1813, the towns people hung lanterns in the tree tops, causing the British to overshoot their mark. Only Cannon Ball House, a two and a half storey brick dwelling was hit in the chimney. This blackout is believed to have been the first in the history of warfare.

The Old Inn at Talbot St. and Mulberry, one of the more interesting buildings, dates to 1816.

The Amelia Welby House was built in the late 18th century. Amelia was born here and wrote poems which won her the praise of Edgar Allan Poe.

The St, Mary's Square Museum displays a restored colonial house, patented in 1659.

The Maritime Museum, dedicated to preserving the culture, crafts and tools of the Bay, is in the shadow of the Hoopers Straight Lighthouse.

Tarr House was built by Edward Elliott, circa 1661. An indentured servant, he helped build the first church at the site of the Episcopal Church.

Barrett's Bed and Breakfast Inn
204 N. Talbot Street
St. Michaels, Md. 21663
(410) 745-3322

the basement, and highlighting the detailed architecture in a Victorian "painted lady" fashion.

The cedar shingles were replaced in the mansard roof and dormer windows.

The entrance hall features a magnificent walnut staircase, which climbs 32 stairs to the third floor mansard. The focal point in the living room (former millinery store) is the antique handcarved oak mantel, which was added to the fireplace. The mantel features a beveled mirror and side columns. The room was repainted to enhance the original wood moldings around the windows and French doors.

The dining room door exits to the open side porch which was replaced, featuring new columns, reproduced to match those on the front porch, and custom made "pineapple" balusters, which are found on many of Oxford's old porches.

The old carriage house at the back of the property has been renovated to provide charming guest quarters in a beautiful Victorian garden setting. Year-round accommodationas are available by calling The Nichols House at (410) 226-5799.

Plimhimmon

Plimhimmon off Oxford Road is the ancestral home of Tench Tilghman and his wife Anna Maria. The land grant was in 1659. It was a one storey home, named after a mountain in Wales by a Welsh owner, Captain Coward. Tench acquired it later as a wedding gift. He is famous for carrying the message of Cornwallis' surrender.

The land and house have been in the Myers family since 1870 when General Tench Tilghman, grandson of the Revolutionary War hero Lieutenant Colonel, had it. Mr. Myers, who still farms the land at 82,

Long Point

Between St. Michaels and Tilghman down a long road is Neavitt. Southwest of it stands Long Point, built by Ralph Elston in 1681. It is believed that he built the existing brick house over the foundations of an earlier structure.(1)

The structure is two stories high with an attic, gambrel roof and dormer windows. The handmade, whitewashed bricks are much larger than usual. The door is flanked by a window on either side. The interior is one big room and originally had fireplaces at each end. Only one remains with a handcarved mantel. A winding stairway twists over the fireplace to the rooms above. The ends of the room are similarly panelled with a cupboard to the right and on the left, the door is cut through to the modern portion.

Ralph Elston married Mary, widow of John Ball in 1694. Lieutenant Thomas Ball,   in 1772, left Long Point to his children, John and Mary.

The current owners have restored it for their parents and preserve it lovingly as "the Cottage" near the water. It is privately owned and not open to the public.

Wye House

Wye House, seat of the famous Lloyd family, is situated where Shaw Bay and Lloyd Creek empty into the Wye River. In colonial times, ocean going sailing vessels could enter the creek, and trade with the" Mother Country" was conducted here.

The first Lloyd, Edward, came to Virginia probably from the Wye Valley of England and Wales. By 1636, he sat on the Virginia House of Burgesses. Circa 1649, he led a group of Puritans from Virginia to Maryland and became a member of the General Assembly in Anne Arundel County.

About 1660, he moved to Talbot County, since the bulk of his holdings were there.

He met Richard Bennett one of the wealthiest land owners of Talbot County. The younger Richard died and his widow married Philemon Lloyd, Edward's son. Edward Lloyd returned to England leaving Philemon to manage the Maryland concerns.(2.) "Madam Lloyd", was the daughter of Captain James Neale and Anna Gill, a lady-in-waiting to King Charles I's Queen, Henrietta Maria, for whom the Colony of Maryland, and the daughter of Anna Gill Neale, are named. Philemon Lloyd and his wife lived on the Wye tract and occupied the original Wye House.

In 1685, Philemon predeceased his father, who died in 1695 and willed Wye House to Philemon's eldest son, the second Edward Lloyd.(3.) Thus began 200 years of Edward Lloyds holding public office and involving himself in public affairs. Edward II married a Quaker girl named Sarah Covington and he, died young, leaving as his heir, his minor son, Edward III who married Ann Rousby of Calvert County Their monuments are to be seen in the Wye Graveyard, one of the largest family cemeteries in the State. Among a number of graves which date from 1684, is that of Admiral Franklin Buchanan, first Superintendent of the Naval Academy. Admiral Buchanan married Ann Catherine, daughter of the fifth

Edward Lloyd, and owned a nearby house called "The Rest".

The present house was erected somewhat previous to 1792, by the fourth Edward Lloyd, who also completed the Chase-Lloyd House in Annapolis. His wife was Eizabeth Tayloe, and the portrait of his brother, Richard Bennett Lloyd hangs in the Wye House dining room. Their youngest daughter, Mary Tayloe Lloyd, married Francis Scott Key.

The fifth Edward Lloyd, Governor of Maryland and a United States Senator in the early 19th century, married Sally Scott Murray, daughter of Dr. James Murray of Annapolis.

The magnificent house and surrounding farmland are owned by a devoted member of the eleventh generation of Lloyds. Dr. and Mrs. R. Carmichael Tilghman, were kind enough to show this writer the house and grounds. On a window pane is scratched the names of Edward and Elizabeth Lloyd, 1792.

The interiors of Wye reflect the transition from the Georgian period to lighter Federal style.(2.)

Wye House is divided into two axis, one from south to north running the width of the building through the front door to the huge north parlor. The other runs the length of the house, west to east to the library on the left and laundry on the right. The kitchen has a bake oven, very modern for the era. The grand house has antiques, 90 percent of which have always belonged to the family.

The palatial dining room with its long castle-like table opens on the hall and also into the north parlor. For large parties, they extended the table through the doorway. The north parlor was called a ballroom. Both rooms have fireplaces, and a lovely tall screened-in porch runs the length of the center section, looking out on the Orangery and gardens, in the center of which was once a bowling green.

One of the most noted buildings on the Wye property is the orangery, the only original one still standing intact in the nation. It has a second story used as a billiard room with an outside stair, and was heated to keep the orange plants warm. Out of line with the house, the center section dates to 1745.

The road leading to the house, lined with oaks and beeches, becomes circular near the striking facade. This example of Palladian architecture was in five parts, but an attached room was added on each end, forming an unusual seven part house. The portico and a large porch on the garden front were added about 1805.

During my conversation with him, just after his 91st birthday, Dr. Tilghman called my attention to the "Ha Ha", a deep ditch, faced with brick, across which cattle would not go. These allowed a fenceless view of rolling lawns and magnificent old trees.

Of the original house, a wing known as the Captain's House", is still standing. The late J. Donnell Tilghman has written that "the records of Talbot County show that court was held in June of 1663, at the house of Edward Lloyd. It is possible that court was held in this building." (J. Donnell Tilghman, "Wye House"in Maryland Historical Magazine, Vol.

47, No. 2.,1953,91.). The Tilghmans and Lloyds are descended from King Edward III, but espoused the patriot cause. They gave a party for Frederick Douglas, who had been a slave at Wye House, to celebrate his fame. The orator toasted the longevity of the Lloyds.(Ibid.) Wye House is not open to the public.

Tilghman Island

Tilghman Island awaits you in serene tranquility, a quaint waterman's island, between the Bay and the Choptank River. You can completely relax, enjoying unspoiled natural beauty of the island.

Go on a sailing excursion in the home of the largest fleet of skipjacks in the nation. First charted by Capt. John Smith in 1608, the island has been inhabited by brave men and women who pioneered the seafood business.

The name Tilghman Island was derived in 1775 by owner Matthew Tilghman. The island suffered a substantial loss of resources in the War of 1812. Steamboat service was established in 1890 and travelers were escorted by horse drawn vehicles, a service now offered by vans. Many accommodations are luxurious and cordiality awaits you everywhere.

Sinclair House Bed and Breakfast
P.O. Box 145
5718 Black Walnut Point Rd.
Tilghman, Md. 21671
(410) 886-2147

Tilghman Island Inn
Coopertown Rd.
Tilghman Island, Maryland 21671
800-336-0592 or 410-886-2141

Harrison's Chesapeake House

Ten years after the guns of the Civil war fell silent, Harrisons Chesapeake Inn entertained their first guests. With over a century of cordial hospitality behind it, the old country inn on Tilghman Island has gained acclaim far and wide for its excellent sports fishing, fine lodging and delicious seafood, served family style.

Family interest has been a key word for four generations of Harrisons at the Chesapeake House. Three generations still operate the house: Miss Alice, 2nd generation, Levin F. III (Buddy) Roberta L. (Bobbie), 3rd generation and Levin F. IV Bud and Charles R. Harrison (Chuck) 4th generation.

Their charter fleet has become the largest privately owned fishing fleet in the nation, and the inn has gained renown for comfortable lodging and fine fare. The oldest portion was built in 1856. Dine over-

looking the famous Choptank River, scene of James A. Michener's *Chesapeake.*

This tradition began in the 1890's when the only water transportation to Baltimore was by steamboat and Buddy's grandfather, Capt. Levin F. (Buddy) Harrison Sr. was a captain in the summers. After docking in Baltimore, he would be asked if there might be some place on the shore where city dwellers could escape the heat. Buddy's grandmother, Ida, a school teacher, didn't teach in the summer. So, her husband started to bring boarders, mainly ladies and children, who left whenever the steamboat came back up the Bay. They were always picked up and delivered back to the boat by horse and buggy, driven most often by Levin F. Harrison, Jr., Buddy's father.

In the early 1900's, the men started coming with their families, but weren't content to just sit in the swings, thus, the fishing business evolved. Then, after the Bay Bridge was built in the 50's, the Baltimore fishing customers started driving their families to enjoy the Harrison's famous seafood. Buddy says that this was the beginning of their restaurant business.

He also advises that all dinners are made to order and that if you're in a hurry, just ask for those items that take the least time. With his easy smile, he says, "Remember, the difference between eating and dining is only a short wait." Pass around fresh vegetables, apple sauce and homemade bread. Then, try the Chesapeake House specialty: Crisp fried chicken and large moist crab cakes. The Harrisons have almost always been in the seafood business. Looking out the tall windows of the Chesapeake House while eating luscious, plump oysters brought in on skipjacks we watch, we remember to savor this moment in time. Since it takes much time and work to catch and prepare fine seafood, we should appreciate these gifts of nature and human patience. The Harrisons hope that you will relax with them because they love to please and see smiling faces, as Buddy phrases it saying, "Find peace in a violent world; go fishing and make friends". He wrote the following:" These days, Harrison's Chesapeake House, overlooking the famous Choptank River, is a pleasant blend of the old and new. Skipjacks are tied up alongside sleek charter and pleasure boats just outside the window of the dining room. Traditional crab cakes share the menu with the finest prime ribs. The informal dining room features many tables by the windows and an inviting fireplace. service is casually efficient and the food is just wonderful!" For reservations, call 410-886-2121.

Moorings

At The Moorings you can savor the essence of the Eastern Shore's timeless spell. Dock among the rushes and stroll up over the meadows in a place where time stands still. Or take a leisurely drive past St. Michaels on Rte 33 onto the old Bay Hundred peninsula, where land opens to water stretching out to the Chesapeake bay on the west and to Harris Creek and the Choptank River on the east. Try your hand at crabbing or fishing from the pier or row out into Waterhole Cove and explore where Blue Heron and deer abound. If the mood strikes you, spend time visiting the shops, museums, antique stores and fine restaurants of nearby towns. Then come home to The Moorings and relax.

The Moorings is a yellow, restored circa 1905 farm house, nestled in 40 acres of waterfront, with a swing, rocking chair and wheel barrow on the front porch. The living room offers a moss green and peach motif with bookcases and charming touches. One bedroom has a fireplace and queen size bed on the ground floor.

The family style kitchen looks out on a sparkling swimming pool to the water beyond. Full breakfasts, in the country manner get your day started right with home made breads, Eggs Moorings, pancakes, waffles and a great cup of coffee. Call l-800/316-6396 for reservations and escape your cares amidst warm hospitality and complete tranquility.

Eggs Moorings
16 slices of white bread, crust trimmed, cubed
1 lb. sharp cheddar cheese, grated
1 1/2 cup Swiss cheese, grated

6 eggs	1 lb. ham, cube
3 cups of milk	1/2 tsp onion salt
3 cups of corn flakes	1 stick of butter

Layer half of bread cubes, ham and cheese in 9 x 13 baking dish, then layer remaining cubes and cheese. Beat eggs in bowl, add milk and seasonings. Pour over layers. Chill over night. When ready to bake, melt butter and combine in bowl with corn flakes. Sprinkle over layers. Bake at 375 degrees for 40 minutes.

Dorchester County

Secluded Dorchester County lies halfway down the Delmarva Peninsula. People on the Western Shore may only know it from the town of Cambridge which they whiz past on the way to Ocean City. This county holds unexplored treasures of history.

In the mid-17th century, the county of Dorset, named for the 4th Earl of Dorset, was established, and the town of Cambridge was founded as its county seat in 1687.

At the head of Gary's Creek stands Spocott Windmill, a working reconstruction of a mill with a miller's house nearby.

The Dorchester Heritage Museum is in the old DuPont airdrome at Horn Point. It features artifacts from an archeological dig, Native American, waterman's and early aviation memorabilia.

Christ Episcopal Church on historic High street in Cambridge is the third church building on its site. The original, constructed in 1693, has a graveyard, holding the remains of Revolutionary War heroes and four of the six governors that Dorchester bestowed upon Maryland. Across the street is the court house, built in 1852.

The "Meredith House", built about 1760, is the home of the Historical Society, furnished in period antiques with artifacts of history and the six Maryland governors born here. On the property is the Neild Museum, which houses farm and Native American artifacts.

The Brannock Maritime Museum, set in a park-like setting of gardens and trees, features artifacts, photographs, tools, instruments and models highlighting Dorchester's role in the maritime history of the Bay.

Dorchester County was once the retirement home of sharp-shooter Annie Oakley.

Harriet Tubman, born a slave on Green Briar Road in South Dorchester, escaped, herself, she worked in assisting slaves to escape via the underground railroad.

The charming village of East New Market established about 1660. provides a walking tour of houses.

Commodor's Cottage Bed & Breakfast
215 Glenburn Avenue
Cambridge, Md. 21613
1-800-228-6938 or (410) 228-6938

Glasgow

At 1500 Hambrooks Boulevard, on the waterfront of Cambridge is Glasgow, the ancestral home of the Tubman family. Dr. Robert F. Tubman purchased the property on July 14, 1842.

Born at St. Giles Fields, May 7, 1791, he graduated from the University of Pennsylvania and practiced at Medicine Hall. He died Christmas Eve, 1864, willing Glasgow to his youngest son, Robert Constantine Tubman, who died in 1916.

Robert researched the house and his own family. He learned that in 1760, William Murray Ward of the Clan Murray in Scotland came to Maryland and purchased the tract of land known as "Ayreshire" and renamed it "Glasgow" after his native city. It was built in that year with thick walls of English brick, painted white. The one-and-a-half storey wing built in 1881 is of white clapboard.

The front door opens on a hall and the stairway on the right, rises in two flights. At the foot of the stairs on the left is a spacious guest room and down the hall is the drawing room. Both rooms give onto the modern porch and have fireplaces. The hall has a carved arch in two parts. The spacious dining room is entered by a door on the right of the hall and is panelled to the ceiling.

This elegant room opens into the kitchen and hall with a flight of stairs which led to the servants quarters. A pantry is further down the hall.

On the National Register, the aristocratic house has meaning in history. William Van Murray, who studied law in England and was Minister to Holland in 1800, was one of the negotiators of the treaty with France which laid the foundation for the Louisiana Purchase. He served in the Second Third and Fourth Congress and died in 1803. His sister Henrietta Murray inherited Glasgow. She and her husband Dr. George I. Robertson sold it to Dr. Robert Tubman. It remained in the Tubman family another 10 years.

The present owners have preserved the home lovingly as a B & B and have seven guest rooms in the house and a new Williamsburg Cottage on the grounds. Please call (410) 228-0575 or 800-373-7890 for reservations.

Vienna, located on the tidewater shores of the Nanticoke River in Dorchester County, is a town nearly untouched by time. One of the oldest settlements in Maryland, its region was first mentioned by Captain John Smith during his exploration of the Nanticoke River in 1608. A settlement already occupied this area in 1669, when Dorchester County was formed. In 1671, the Colonial Assembly recommended this point as a ferry location, and Vienna was formally founded in 1706. Jacob Lockerman, the clerk of the committee, appointed to lay out the town, suggested the name Vienna, following the practice of naming towns after those in Europe.

Photograph by Marion E. Warren

The Tavern House

The Tavern House on Water Street predates 1800 and has always been a focal point of Vienna. During the colonial period, it was a tavern as its name implies, a place where travelers could find food and lodging as they traveled down the Delaware peninsula. Today it continues this role of providing hospitality to travelers as a bed and breakfast, under the ownership of the Altergotts, a cordial couple, knowledgeable about local history.

Alexander Laine was one of the early innkeepers during the 1760's, and Alexander Douglas was both innkeeper and postmaster in the 1790's. He operated a ferry, which crossed the Nanticoke River at Vienna and with Jim Smoot, built the first bridge across it, Unfortunately sailing ships had trouble passing through the bridge's draw, and it was ordered to be torn down in 1860. Ferry operations were then reestablished and continued through 1931,when a new bridge was built. The last ferry's toll house is now on Race St. where it has served as an office for the local magistrate, then as a Town Hall. Now, it is being used as a meeting place for the Vienna Heritage Commission.

The Tavern House has an unobstructed view of the river and marshes beyond. It is an excellent place to while away time watching osprey, listening to the birds, or appreciating the quiet beauty of the marsh.

The house's architecture is simple colonial. The wide door with its semi-circular fan light above, leads to a foyer, which seems to welcome you back to colonial times. A lovely ship's lantern shines down upon a remarkable Naval sword, and large iron keys hang from pegs on the wall, as one might imagine they hung long ago.

Looking out on the marsh, one cannot help but notice the distorted view provided by the hand blown glass that is to be expected in a colonial tavern.

Above the entrance way is beautifully detailed carving, inside and out, on the chair rails, on fireplace mantles and on the fluted pilasters flanking

eral park benches, a tent-style garden gazebo, a large rope hammock, plus tables and chairs on the brick patio next to the pond.

All in all, the Tavern House would seem to be an ideal place to sample the hospitality and quiet of Maryland's Eastern Shore. Call 410-376-3347.

Worchester County

Worchester County has the lovely Pocomoke River traveling its length to the Bay. In 1742 the county was divided from Somerset, and Snow Hill became the county seat. A walk through this royal port is a stroll through history. Founded by English colonists in 1642, the town was named Snow Hill after a district of London.

Chanceford Hall

In the 17th century town of Snow Hill stands Chanceford. Set back from West Federal Street at 209, this white stuccoed brick home is stately and dignified. It was probably built from 1759 - 1790 and was purchased from Francis Ross by James Rounds Morris, Clerk of the Court of Worcester County.

On the National Register, Chanceford has been well preserved through the years and is an excellent example of a colonial dwelling with a classic exterior. The front door is in the pedimented gable-end, which would usually be the side. It has a full pediment with dentils and a bull's eye window with star pattern in the center, and three small rectangular windows below this round window, which was an unusual arrangement. An exterior panelled door has been added outside the original one to protect it from the elements. Conforming to the shape of the house roof is a shallow overhang roof with dentils, supported by columns.

The front door has a heart-and-star leaded transom over it, and opens into the hall, running the width of the house. Doors are all of two-ply thickness with inner sides laid with stout wooden bars and large locks. The doors to the 15 x 17 foot living room and 15 x 17 foot other living room open off the hall. Each room offers a large fireplace with elegantly designed mantels.

There are ten operating fireplaces in the house. The former ballroom, at one time detached from the main house, is 20 x 22 feet. It was later joined to the larger wing by an addition, now used as the dining room. That former ballroom is now a kitchen. The rear hall also extends the width of the house and has its own staircase, with square reeded balusters, panelling and intricate step-ends. The mantel of the former ballroom was moved into the dining room, where there is an operating fireplace, 3 foot wainscoting about the room and fluted panels under the windows.

the entrance. Walls are the bright white of the sand, lime and hair plaster. Colors of the woodwork are authentic. Tavern House" hues identified by paint analysis: early l8th century grey and the bright blue of the late l700's.

The foyer opens to two rooms, one a dining room and the other a great room, which is really two rooms whose dividing wall has been removed in the past. The doors have iron thumb latches, some with original box locks with wood cases. Three fireplaces give a cozy feeling to the rooms. They are furnished with a variety of items, which somehow complement one another beautifully. Interesting accents from the Altergotts' travels include a Turkish candle powered signal lamp, an 18th century French wall clock and carved Chinese tables.

Upstairs, over the foyer, is a cozy sitting area that looks out over the river and marsh. Also at the top of the stairs is "The River Room" in which the bed backs to a diagonal wall, so that it faces the window and river. The fireplace opening is offset, since its chimney is shared with one downstairs. On the mantle is a large OG clock and flanking the fireplace is a large wing chair which is in sharp contrast to the small doll chair on the other side.

"Hanna's Room", which is next door, is somewhat larger but has the same warm feeling. It, too, has the white sand, lime and hair plaster walls, accented by blue woodwork. This fireplace is also offset and has the smallest fireboxes in the house.

A hall leads past another bedroom to the "new" addition (about l00 years old), at the rear of the house. Character studies of colonial folk enhance the hallway, and old linens lay on a drying rack.

The room at the end of the hall has a Victorian motif, with flowered wall paper, antique twin beds and a large deep red blanket chest. Windows on all three walls look down on the garden with its towering pecan trees, ancient boxwood, and a small pond which is home to gold fish, frogs and waterlilies.

The large yard offers many opportunities for relaxing and possibly sipping libations. There are sev-

In 1970, a solarium was added off the present kitchen, connected by a breezeway to the garage and near a lovely swimming pool.

The second owner of Chanceford was Judge William Whittington, who died there in 1827 and is buried nearby. His son-in-law, Judge William Tingle, inherited. Later, Judge Edward O. Thomas owned it. The Court House is located only a few blocks from the home.

The fine old garden has been reduced, but the old English ivy, brought from Kenilworth, is still verdant.

The congenial owners have restored the house handsomely, and Mr. Driscoll has built the fine kitchen cabinets among other exquisite accents pieces. The house has 10 operating fireplaces and boasts original woodwork, plaster, floors, mantles and much glass.

This is a beautifully preserved example of colonial architecture and a sumptuous bed and breakfast. Call (301) 632-2231 for reservations.

Warren House

The Warren House on Church street in Snow Hill is a magnificent example of a Queen Anne style home built in 1895 by a former governor and two times U.S. Senator. Ray Warren, former mayor, resides here with his vivacious wife, Helen.

The house was the former home of Dr. Albert Cohen, beloved Snow Hill physician whose X Ray machine is still in the small bar formerly his laboratory. His examining room was in the parlor to the left of the ornate front door, which bears a family crest on the transom. Exquisite stained glass panels are repeated throughout the house and are believed to be the work of Tiffany.

The palatial parlor has a beautiful tiled fireplace enhanced by a handsome cherry mantel and bas relief cherubs.

This is a storybook house, white with burgundy shutters and wide wrap-around porches, the kind of house of happy days and wondrous dreams.

River House Inn
201 E. Market St.
Snow Hill, MD 21863
410-632-2722

Somerset County

"Search others for their virtues, thyself for thy vices."
Benjamin Franklin

Somerset County, located on the southernmost portion of Maryland's Eastern Shore, is a masterpiece of nature. It combines tradition and simplicity with beauty of the pristine countryside. History is present here from the famous Ward Brothers' decoy carving to the historic homes of Princess Anne.

Once a busy area for the harvest of oysters and fish, the seafood centers at Crisfield and Deale Island have a charm of simplicity. Crisfield, once called the "Seafood Capital of the World", still offers the J. Millard Tawes Historical Museum, honoring the native son who served as State Governor. You can also enjoy the Smith and Tangier Island Cruises based at Crisfield.

The Washington Hotel

The Washington Hotel is the only hotel in Maryland to be managed continuously as a hotel for 200 years. On Somerset Avenue in the heart of historic Pricess Anne, it is the hub for that town's cultural life.

Historians often speak with Mary A. Murphey, who has owned and operated this old hostelry for some thirty years, having inherited it from her parents.

According to the deed records, it was built in 1744. The walls of the lobby are lined with pictures of all U.S. Presidents and many First Ladies, plus other important documents. An old ledger dates to the 18th century.

The lovely original dining room at the end of the hall has a musket from Civil War days and a sideboard from the mid 18th century. A large spinning wheel is in the hallway near the stairs to guest rooms. The older guest rooms offer antiques, while six remodelled rooms are in a more modern style.

Mrs. Muphey's son, Bob, manages the newer restaurant dining room and coffee shop. The specialties are fine seafood entrees, such as lightly fried Chesapeake Bay Oysters and a marvelous seafood Platter.

During the second weekend in October the town is crowded for its "Princess Anne Days", including tours of historic homes. Some notables are Beckford, built in 1776 by Henry Jackson and the Robertson House.

A visit to the inn can be an intriguing step back into history. This is a genuine treasure for the State, as it was frequented by Samuel Chase and his father, who was born in Princess Anne.

Testimonials include that of a physician, who said he considered the Washington Hotel his "home away from home" and that the owners offered "warm hospitality and extend themselves in order to please".

The hotel has hosted Governor Thomas King Carroll, Governor Levin Winder, and many other famous figures. Call Mrs. Murphey at 301-651-2525.

Teackle Mansion

In Princess Anne stands the Teackle Mansion, an outstanding example of early nineteenth-century architectural design, built in several stages between 1802 and 1818-19 by merchant and statesman, Littleton Dennis Teackle (1777-1848) and his wife.

In 1802 they purchased nine acres of the Beckford plantation, patented in 1681 by Edmond Howard and probably began construction in 1802.

Only the center section and part of the adjacent hyphens were built during 1802. The north and south wings and the hyphens were completed in 1818-19. It has a flemish bond brick facade and highly-ornamented center section.

The design of the building was the result of a trip Mr. Teackle made to Glasgow, Scotland, where he saw a fascinating castle.

In spite of his strong interest in architecture, a professional architect probably oversaw the design and construction of the building. The detail and ornamentation of the Mansion's temple facade, its symmetrical arrangement, and meticulous plasterwork indicate the hand of a professional.

It's most notable architectural features include three decorative plaster panels on the front facade between the first and second storey windows, two interior mirrored windows, and false doors and archways in the front hall and drawing room that help to achieve symmetry. An interior marble-laid bath and underground cistern and a kitchen with large fireplace and beehive oven are other interesting attributes. The estate also had a number of outbuildings, including two houses for servants, a dairy/wash house, and a smoke house, all of which are extant.

Littleton Teackle owned extensive agricultural and timber lands, traded local and imported goods, established the Bank of Somerset in 1813, and served for many years in the Maryland House of Delegates.

In 1839, four years after his wife died, having been in and out of debt most of his life, Littleton Teackle sold the Mansion. He died in 1848.

The Teackle Mansion is now owned by two local historical organizations and is open on a regular basis for guided tours.

(Somerset" An Architectural History, Paul Touart, Maryland Historical Trust and Somerset County Historical Trust, 1990.)

Notes

1. Quotes of Statesmen and Philosophers, Elbert Hubbard, *An American Bible*, The Roycrafters, N.Y., 1911.
2. Cross Manor
1. Regina Hammett, *History of St. Mary's County*, Ridge, Md. 1977.
2. Ibid. 3. Ibid. 4. Ibid.
Don Swann etching
3. Sotterley Plantation
1. Susan Dowell & Marion Warren, *Great Houses of Maryland*, Tidewater Publishers, Centreville, Md. 1988, pg 4.
2. Ibid, pg. 5. 3. Ibid, pg. 6. 4. Ibid, pgs 7 & 8.
5. Ibid, pg. 6. Photo by M.E. Warren
4. Thomas Stone Historic site
1. Don Swann, *Colonial and Historic Homes of Maryland*, Johns Hopkins Press, Balt. 1982
5. Mount Clare Mansion
1. Dowell and Warren, *Great Houses of Maryland*, 86
2. Ibid, 34. 3. Ibid.
Don Swann etching
Hampton Historic Site
1. Dowell and Warren, Great Houses of Maryland, 86
2. Ibid. 86 & 87
3. Ibid. 89 4. Ibid. 86
Don Swann etching
7. Preston on Patuxent
1. Charles Stein, *History of Calvert County*, Calvert Co. Historical Society, 1976, pg.25

2. Ibid.
3. Hulbert Footner, *Charles' Gift*, Harper & Bros., N.Y., 1939.
4. Swann, Colonial and Historic Homes of Maryland, 28.
8. Rousby Hall
1. Stein, *A History of Calvert County*, 25.
9. London Town Publik House
1. Dowell and Warren, *Great Houses of Maryland*, 42
2. Ibid, 44. 3 Ibid, 45. 4. Ibid, 46, 5. Ibid. 6 Ibid, 42.
10. Brice House
1. Robert Bowie Johnson, *Broad Neck Hundred* Vol.III, No. 2, 22. 2. Ibid. 3. Dowell & Warren, 57.
2. Ibid.
11. Little Brice House
12. Paca House
1. Dowell and Warren, *Great Houses of Maryland*, 49.
2. Ibid. 49.
13. Chase Lloyd House
1. Dowell and Warren, 64. 2 Ibid.
14. Hammond Harwood House
1. Dowell and Warren, 78. 2 Ibid.
15. Jonas Green House
1. R. L. Demeter, *Primers, Presses and Composing sticks, Women Printers of the Colonial Era*, Exposition Press, 1979.
2. *A Descriptive History of a House and its Family*, Mary Donya Brown, Graduate Thesis, 1989.
16. Charles Inn

1. Isle of Kent Col Rent Roll
2. Schoch, *Of History and Houses*, Kent Island Heritage Society, Queen Anne press, 1982, Stevensville, 22
3. Ibid, 21. 4. Ibid, 33.
17. History of Quenn Anne's County
1. Robert B. Johnson, *Broad Neck Hundred*, Vol II, No. 2 pg. 3, 4.
18. Kent Manor Inn
1. Schoch, *Of History and Houses*, Kent Island Heritage society, Queen Anne Press, pgs. 58, 59.
2. Kent Island Rent Roll.
19. Hermitage
1. *Colonial Families and Their Descendants*, Queen Anne's County Homemakers, 1938.
20. Hinchingham
1. Swann, *Colonial and Historic Homes*, 138.
1. Ibid.
21. Wye House
1. Christopher Weeks, *Where Land and Water Intertwines*, Johns Hopkins Press, 1984, 53.
2. Ibid. 3. Ibid, 54. 4. Ibid. 5. Op.cit. 6. Ibid.
7. J. Donell Tilghman, "Wye House" in Maryland Historical Magazine, Vol. 47, No 2., 1953, 91.
22. Long Point.
1. Don Swann, *Colonial and Historic Homes of Maryland*, pg. 160.
32. Teakle Mansion
1. Paul Touart, *Somerset County, An Architectural History*, Maryland Historical Trust and Somerset County Historical Trust, 1990.